Scholarly Podca

CW01501747

Exploring what academic podcasting is and what it could be, this book is the first to consider the why, what, and how academics engage with this insurgent, curious craft.

Featuring interviews with 101 podcasting academics, including scholars and teachers of podcasting, this book explores the motivations of scholarly podcasters, interrogates what podcasting does to academic knowledge, and leads potential podcasters through the creation process from beginning to end. With scholarship often trapped inside expensive journals, wrapped in opaque language, and laced with a standoffish tone, this book analyses the implications of moving towards a more open and accessible form.

This book will also inform, inspire, and equip scholars of any discipline, rank, or affiliation who are considering making a podcast or who make podcasts with the background knowledge and technical and conceptual skills needed to produce high-quality podcasts through a reflexive critique of current practices.

Ian M. Cook is the Director of Studies at the Open Learning Initiative (OLIve) at Central European University (CEU). He is part of the Allegra Lab editorial collective.

Scholarly Podcasting
Why, What, How?

Ian M. Cook

Routledge
Taylor & Francis Group

LONDON AND NEW YORK

Cover image: © Gyula Németh

First published 2023
by Routledge
4 Park Square, Milton Park, Abingdon, Oxon OX14 4RN

and by Routledge
605 Third Avenue, New York, NY 10158

Routledge is an imprint of the Taylor & Francis Group, an informa business

© 2023 Ian M. Cook

British Library Cataloguing-in-Publication Data
A catalogue record for this book is available from the British Library

ISBN: 978-0-367-43942-2 (hbk)
ISBN: 978-0-367-43944-6 (pbk)
ISBN: 978-1-003-00659-6 (ebk)

DOI: 10.4324/9781003006596

Typeset in Times New Roman
by SPi Technologies India Pvt Ltd (Straive)

Access the Support Material: www.routledge.com/9780367439446

For Máté
(insurgent, curious, and crafty)

Contents

Extended Table of Contents

Introduction

What is this book of curated quotes in your hands? It's an attempt to understand why, what, and how scholars podcast.

1 Why? Because It's Insurgent

Scholarly podcasting is an insurgency against academic structures that curb creativity, inhibit personal and collective transformations, and promote self-interest over generosity.

1.1 Creative

Part of this insurgency is built on the creativity that emerges from a podcasting practice that works out what it is or could be as it goes along. Unlike much text-based scholarship which is aloof and authoritative, podcasting has a register which is intimate and vulnerable, something that invites pedagogical innovation.

The **intimate** register of scholarly podcasting is engendered through listening practices (earbuds that penetrate the body), listening choices (active subscription), and also the ways in which the closeness of the medium allows for expression of emotions as scholars speak.

Vulnerability emerges when scholars transparently talk through the methods that led them to their conclusions, improvise or test out unfinished ideas, come into dialogue with divergent voices, and embrace an unauthoritative mode of being a scholar. Teachers can embrace the intimacy and vulnerability afforded by podcasting in their **pedagogies** by creating course lectures or relevant conversations, or helping students create public-facing work.

1.2 Transformative

Scholarly podcasting's insurgency is transformative. It's transformative within everyday scholarly life, as it offers potential intellectual freedom for those academics who thirst for alternative ways to be scholars; it's personally transformative as it upskills those who practise it; and it's transformative of academic careers as it becomes increasingly recognised and rewarded by institutions.

Because no one is sure what scholarly podcasting practice is or could be, it is **freeing** for those who embrace it. Podcasting allows a form of scholarly life that values academics beyond the number of publications they have, facilitates the search for meaning and joy at workplaces that seem uncaring, and challenges the demarcations of what is and is not 'scholarly'. It transforms individual scholars through an **upskilling** of their reading, writing, listening, and speaking practices that then feed into their teaching and other work. And it can be **rewarding** in the workplace as it is increasingly recognised and understood by peers and institutions, leading to jobs and promotions (directly and indirectly), as well as providing opportunities for networking and personal promotion.

1.3 Generous

Scholarly podcasting's insurgency is a generous one: it opens up scholarship in a free and accessible way, cultivates relationships with listeners over time that are both narrow and deep, and creates communities of scholars that are askew to existing academic structures.

It is a practice of **opening scholarship** through the inclusion of diverse and divergent voices and by putting scholarship back into communities in a way that allows methods and assumptions to be challenged by publics (because scholarship is presented in a nuanced, complex yet accessible fashion). It is also a way of **cultivating listenership** with ongoing interactions and feelings of togetherness forged with publics and peers as fields of study are both impacted and commented upon. And scholarly podcasting helps the **creation of communities** as new and alternate voices are heard and friendships are formed.

2 What? A Curiosity Generator

The creative, transformative, and generous practice of scholarly podcasting helps create the conditions for scholars to follow their curiosity. Scholarly podcasts are thus curiosity feeders and, because they open up possible avenues of interest as they go, they are also curiosity generators that provoke changes in ways of asking, forms of knowledge production, and modes of knowledge creation.

2.1 A Way of Asking

Podcasts engender changes in ways of asking: conversations are dynamically animated; scholarship is alive with engaged storytelling; and listeners actively fill in the gaps.

Podcasts with **dynamic conversations** have questions that lead to new thoughts that lead to new questions that lead to new thoughts as discussions deepen and knowledge is picked over or produced. Podcasts with **engaged storytelling** both entertain and inform through crafted audio narratives or conversations. And podcasts with deliberate spaces invite **active listening**, where consumers deep dive into complex subjects, letting their imaginations roam within and through sonic indeterminacies.

2.2 A Form of Publishing

Curiosity can be followed and generated through forms of publishing in which there are fewer gatekeepers, but this calls for new forms of evaluation, something further challenged by the presence of voices (which bring their own affordances and complications).

Publishing **without gatekeepers** allows for immediate publishing and deep dives into complex topics, but this also calls into question scholarly authority. It is thus unsurprising that many are **asking for evaluation** of scholarly podcasts, including through new forms of peer review. Because **voices are present** within podcasts, traditional review models are challenged, but these voices also bring a set of possibilities for openings and closures as listeners hear excitement, accents, inflection, identity, and more.

2.3 A Mode of Knowledge Creation

Scholarly podcasts can, for some disciplines, be modes of knowledge creation acting as data collection, thinking tools, or as a key component within a wider process or project.

When conceived within a research project as **data collection**, the practice of podcasting can be the research itself, especially when sound or talking is central, or when interviewees are reluctant to give 'standard' academic interviews. Scholarly podcasting can also be a **tool for thinking** as conversations allow for sensemaking or concept development, whilst reading and listening more widely creates new linkages between seemingly disparate ideas. And scholarly podcasting can also be conceived of as **part of a process**: the spark or development of an idea that leads to a chapter, article, or book, the means to work through complex ideas or shift one's opinions, and the means of keeping research alive through new cycles of reflection and commentary.

3 How? With Craft

The craft of scholarly podcasting should be appreciated, understood, and developed. There are (at least) 11 steps on this journey.

3.1 Create…

An idea that draws on the unique affordances of podcasting.

3.2 Listen…

To loads of podcasts so as to better understand structure.

3.3 Structure…

The elements of your show in an order that best communicates your ideas.

3.4 Develop…

Your series by thinking through if and how your individual episodes can be linked.

3.5 Write…

For the ear and not the eye, in a clear and lively manner.

3.6 Speak…

With your voice, which you can use to convey certain meanings to particular audiences.

3.7 Interview…

For tape with preparation, crafted questions, and an audience in mind.

Acknowledgements

I first began making scholarly podcasts in Aberdeen in 2015. My podcast-hating partner had begun a research project there, and so I found myself in a really expensive town, far from home without any friends or scholarly community. And I had a PhD dissertation to write. So naturally, rather than take this perfect opportunity to write a lot, I responded to a call by the New Books Network (NBN) founder Marshall Poe to become the new host of New Books in South Asian Studies. Like all dealers in addictive substances, Marshall and the NBN team created a gateway – I didn't have to worry about any of the technical side; I just had to write to authors, get a copy of their book, and chat with them, before passing on the files to NBN. After a while, I didn't even need to contact authors as they started to contact me.

Less than a year later, with a few score podcasts under my belt and a newborn on my back, I slipped further into an addict's life; I found myself in a darkened room in Budapest listening to hours of podcasts and reading piles of books whilst rocking a baby and praying he'd sleep. A year or so later, freshly unemployed after defending my PhD at the Central European University (CEU), I was having a beer or five with the needlessly critical Dumitriţa Holdiş. She said, 'your podcasts could be better'; I said, 'could you do better?'; we said, 'we should write a grant to upskill ourselves and the university at large'. And so, we wrote two internal grants at CEU.

The first 'Academic Podcasting: Digital Scholarship, Communities of Knowledge Production and the Elusive Search for the Public' was hosted by CEU's Centre for Media Data and Society (CMDS), where I remain a Fellow. It was here I first began to research scholarly podcasts and benefitted from the amazing institutional support for this whole endeavour. Eva Bognar and Marius Dragomir at CMDS were endlessly supportive of the project, and its sprawling never-quite-completed nature. I think I still owe a research deliverable from that first grant, which I guess/ hope is this book. Sorry/thanks.

We then expanded to have the work funded by CEU's Intellectual Themes Initiative, with the project 'Sound Relations – Transgressions, Disruptions, Transformations', in which we broadened the scope to sound studies, taught a lot of scholarly podcast workshops, set up CEU's podcast library, built its first podcast studio, and started thinking seriously about the intersection of pedagogy and audio technology under the wise guidance of Helga Dorner.

Parallel to all this, one of the authors whom I interviewed for New Books in South Asian Studies, media anthropologist Sahana Udupa, had just got funding for a new project about online media and politics in India. She asked if I'd like to join her team to create a podcast, I said, 'of course/how much?' and so we co-hosted 'Online Gods – Digital Cultures in India and Beyond' for a couple of brilliant years, exploring how digitalisation is changing public spheres in India. It was great fun, and I learnt a lot about how to think about digital media, which proved invaluable for this book.

As that podcast series was coming to an end, I began working on the urban environmental justice project UrbanA. Like all addicts who don't know how to suggest anything else apart from ways to feed their addiction, I said, 'let's make a podcast' at some point or another. I soon began making 'Urban Arena – A Podcast about Sustainable and Just Cities' together with the indefatigable Kate McGinn. We laughed a lot.

This book would not have been possible without the wonderful opportunities to make podcasts with all of these wonderful co-hosts/enablers. It also would not have been possible without the foresight of Sarah Hyde, Commissioning Editor at Routledge. She read a short piece I wrote for THE about the Voice Matters podcast series we ran at OLIve Weekend Program, a university education initiative for learners who have experienced displacement (where I now work as Director of Studies). She set up a call and suggested that I submit a book proposal. As I spectacularly missed all of the deadlines we agreed upon for the manuscript, I only cursed her lightly, for which I am as sorry as she is patient.

One of the good things about being so late was that by the time I got round to interviewing people, the world had gone into lockdown. This meant I found a lot of scholars who were stuck at home and were willing to talk to me. It's standard for people to thank all those they interviewed when doing research, but in this case, as you'll see when you start reading, their words are so central to everything: there really would not have been a book without them. A million thanks to each and every podcaster I spoke with; you were so astute, articulate, and insightful that I want this book to be five times as long.

And another thing I want is a different way for people interested in scholarly things to have a scholarly life. Podcasting is a bit of this for me, but so is being part of the radically optimist anthropology platform Allegra Lab. Not only is it a great way to explore the promise of scholarly podcasting, like we did with The Corona Diaries and do with ResonanceCast, but it's also a constant source of critical comradeship and support.

I was inspired to think differently about the review progress of this book, in part because of the critically experimental shenanigans at Allegra Lab but also because of a multi-year conversation with Lori Beckstead and Hannah McGregor about podcasting and peer review for a book we're writing on the topic. And so, I decided to open up this book for 'mass peer review' for a fortnight or so to see what would happen. And the following people jumped in to give comments, suggestions, and feedback: Rik Adriaans, Thomas Aichinger, Judith Beyer, Kate Coyer, Roni Dorot, Zoltán Dujisin, Felix Girke, Dumitriţa Holdiş, Michele Lobo, Otávio Mattos, Jovan Maud, St. John McKay, Bruno Ricardo Faustino Mesquita, Olea Morris, Marion Parish, Jenny Rodriguez, Alexandra Szőke, Erzsébet Strausz, Pooja Venkatesh, and Lucia Udvardyova. They are wonderful people and I thank them very much.

Talking of wonderful people, I could not have done any of this without the love of my dear wife Alexa. Even if she has never listened to a single podcast I have ever made. In spite of this (or maybe because of it), we did manage to make a son together, and his insurgent, curious, crafty nature has been a deep well of inspiration from the very start of my podcasting journey.

1 Introduction

In this book I make the case that scholarly podcasting is an insurgent, curious craft. I do so by drawing on interviews with 101 podcasting academics, including scholars and teachers of podcasting.

I claim that for many scholars podcasting is an insurgency against academic structures that curb creativity, inhibit personal and collective transformations, and promote self-interest over generosity. I further argue that the creative, transformative, and generous practice of scholarly podcasting helps create the conditions for scholars to be immersed in their curiosity. The practice of making scholarly podcasts is one of curiosity generation – it allows scholars to follow where their curiosity takes them and, as they do so, new pathways for their curiosity to flow are created. Such practices provoke changes in ways of asking, forms of scholarly publication, and modes of knowledge creation, at least when they are done well, and doing it well requires an engagement with the craft of podcasting.

The purpose of the book is, to put it bluntly, to do scholarship better. I understand that the current conditions within which many scholars operate is one that is consumed by rankings, preoccupation with prestige, individualism, and careerism. I don't want to judge people for the choices they make to do research within such constraints,

DOI: 10.4324/9781003006596-1

but I do wish to find a way to engage in scholarly inquiry in a more generous, creative, and hopefully transformative manner. Podcasting is one way to do this, I believe, because it allows curiosity to sit at the heart of knowledge creation, publishing forms, and methods of inquiry.

As such, this book is for scholars and students of any discipline, rank, or affiliation who are considering making a podcast or who make podcasts; it is meant to inspire good scholarly podcasting through a reflexive critique of current practices. The book is also for those interested in podcast studies, higher education studies, media studies, questions of knowledge production, and more.

I am a social anthropologist by training, but I have actively tried to avoid using my discipline's language so as to make the book as accessible as possible (though I cannot deny that the choices I made in research design and so on were naturally influenced by my disciplinary background).

In doing the research, I was pushed to think a lot about academic knowledge production, especially scholarly writing norms, and what I could possibly learn from podcasting. At some point during the middle of the writing process, I decided to remove nearly all of my own words and place the rich, articulate, and reflexive thoughts of the podcasters front and centre; they know how to speak well because they podcast (or they were drawn to podcasting because they speak well). The book was subjected to a wonderful 'mass public peer review', in which 20 generous people gave feedback on the manuscript. Nearly all of these kind reviewers asked that I put a bit more of myself into the book at the start of each section, which I have done in a way that is inspired by the practices of podcast hosts I like – introduce a topic, make connections, ask a question, and let the conversation flow with gentle direction.

The book is still mostly interviews, however. They have been transcribed, analysed, and curated in a way that I hope convinces you that scholarly podcasting is an insurgent practice for many scholars, a generator of curiosity for those who make and listen to them, and a craft whose affordances should be appreciated. Because the book is an act of curation rather than assertion, I make the argument in, I hope, a subtle, nuanced, multi-faceted, and productively contrasting fashion. But I understand that this might not be to everyone's taste. With this in mind, I have also presented 'the argument' in the Extended Table of Contents, which you may have already glanced at, so as to guide you along the way. The reading and theorisation I undertook, which informs the research design and analysis, lie gently across the book; I leave a more traditional 'scholarly' theorisation for a more suitable outlet.

I hope this writing choice will be embraced by you. Of course, it's possible to make many arguments for 'standard' academic writing, however, in reflecting on what I love about good podcasts – their contingency, their vulnerability, their experimentation – I decided to let the content suggest this form.

I was drawn to do this because I became aware that a combination of years of speed-reading academic texts for narrow purposes, and skim-reading digital media for shallow entertainment, has made me a much worse reader than I used to be. I skip over long quotes and jump to the end of articles. I miss the immersion within texts that used to bring me joy as a reader. At the same time, through listening to and making a lot of podcasts I have become, I think, a much better listener because when I listen I slow down and lean into the content.

As such, I invite you to read this book deeply, even if you have been conditioned otherwise. In what follows you will have to read the quotes or you will have little else to read. You will engage with the book's argument, I hope, in a slow, thoughtful, and appreciative manner guided by my curation of the interviews. I think it works best from front to back because the quotes are arranged to be in dialogue with each other, but you can jump around if you want to. The excerpts used are not exact word-for-word transcripts of what the podcasters said in conversation but rather readable, faithful representations of what was said in text form. The audio selection that accompanies this book is thus slightly different from the written version, because the voices are edited so they are listenable rather than readable.

When I first began this research project, I set out to find out why scholars podcast, what scholars podcast, and how scholars podcast. Aside from the 101 interviews, I also listened to at least three episodes of each podcast series (if I could understand the language) and drew on my own experience as a podcaster, teacher, and co-founder of a university-based podcasting initiative.

I selected the podcasts through a public call (social media and email lists) and followed this up with a snowball method and a targeted approach as I sought podcasts from disciplines that were underrepresented in the initial stage. We spoke online, usually for around an hour via Zoom or something similar, and I got the impression that for most of the people I spoke with it was the first time they had reflected on their podcasting practice. I sent a list of topics I would discuss in advance, but the discussions themselves were also dependent on my reflections from listening to their work and also moved around as all generative conversations do.

The sample reflects my language skills and disciplinary bias (so please do not get angry if your favourite academic podcast was not featured, or if you make a scholarly podcast I was not aware of). Not all of the podcasters interviewed would consider themselves to be scholars (some are journalists and some are ex-academics), but I wanted to understand processes of translation from 'traditional scholarship' into different podcast forms. Similarly, not all of the podcasts would be considered 'scholarly' by the scholars who made them (some consider them to be fun or fluffy), but I wanted to understand how scholars translated their work into differently accessible content.

There's a lot of diversity within scholarly podcasts besides obvious disciplinary or topic-based differences.

There's diversity in format: some are a limited series, whilst others are ongoing and open ended. There's diversity in the elements used: some are based around interviews and discussions, or focus on narration or documentary-style storytelling, whilst some are recordings of lectures or events. And there's a diversity in purpose: some are used to think through ideas, network, or upskill, whilst others aim to disseminate knowledge, educate, speak to publics, gather data, teach students, or change academia (or a mixture of these). This diversity was represented in the research. Though there is certainly a case for focusing on certain styles of scholarly podcasting or the particular reasons for scholarly podcasting in future research, this particular book is about the broad phenomena of scholarly podcasts made by academics, students, or those adjacent to academia.

I wanted to undertake the research because of the sudden explosion in scholarly podcasting. At the beginning of the project, I futilely attempted to map academic podcasts, but they were being created faster than I could track them. It is not, of course, the final word on scholarly podcasting, though it is the first book of its kind. As such, the reach is wide, and there are multiple invitations for deeper dives into many of the subjects raised. It cannot be comprehensive, nor does it aspire to be. There is a fast-growing podcast studies field of research, and I have referred to many excellent publications in the references, even though the style of the book led me not to use their words directly in the text.

Some may suggest that scholarly podcasting is an obscure or unimportant topic for a book, but I would disagree. What's at stake are crucial questions about who produces scholarship, and who interacts with and critiques it. It raises fundamental questions around the democratisation of access to knowledge, the rising plurality of media production, and the role of scholars within these processes. This is not an inward-facing book that examines the ways a few academics operate. It's an outward-facing book that calls on my fellow scholars and any future scholars to follow their curiosity, perfect their craft, and launch an insurgency against anyone or anything that stops scholarly podcasting from reaching its full potential!

2   Why? Because It's Insurgent

Scholarly podcasting is an insurgency against academic structures that curb creativity, inhibit personal and collective transformations, and promote self-interest over generosity.

> 01:18:06,000 You've just put your finger on something there. There's a solidarity or camaraderie among academic podcasters because we all know there's something we're trying to fix here. We might not be able to say what that is, but there's something driving us to do this.
>
> **Nicholas Kiersey, Fully Automated**

> 00:14:10,000 I think that academia spends its time being like, 'oh, there goes that thing' and not grabbing it and not doing it. And being like, 'what did we do 10 years ago? Let's do that now'.
>
> **Place + Space Collective, Acadammit Podcast**

> 00:21:52,000 I'm not sure it's always clear whether our podcast is academic production or production of an academic [laughs].
>
> **Liz Wayne, PhDivas Podcast**

DOI: 10.4324/9781003006596-2

Creative

Intimate

I've found myself in the bath with cold knees on a lazy Sunday afternoon, laying next to my sleeping partner at home, cradling a sleeping newborn baby in a mildew-riddled flat in Aberdeen, and in Lidl at checkout 12 trying to remember why I was there and what I was meant to do, all whilst immersed in scholarly conversations on topics that, a decade or so earlier, I would have only heard in universities or at select times on BBC Radio 4. But the possibility to hear people speak about these topics was dependent on the choices of university departments and commissioning editors; the tenor of delivery was often serious and restrained, and whether the voice was coming from a radio's speaker or a lecture hall's stage, I often felt distanced from what was happening, even if it was live and invited questions or comments.

I didn't conceptualise it at the time, but what drew me to listening to scholarly and other podcasts was a form of intimacy. It reminded me, in many ways, of how I used to listen to taped radio plays alone in my room as a child, the sort of mediated alone time which you search for in a terraced house with two loud sisters, and which, as I grew older and started to share domestic spaces with friends and partners, was lost to communal media consumption or private music listening. Scholarly podcasting, in part, was about creating intimate listening experiences – engendered through headphones and subscriptions – in which joy, excitement, and sorrow could be heard in scholarly pursuits.

Why does scholarly podcasting feel so intimate?

> 00:46:35,000 Think about that you're most often quite literally in someone's ears. You fill their head with the sound of your voice, or the story that you're telling, or the experiences you're trying to introduce them to.
> **Bonni Stachowiak, Teaching in Higher Ed**

00:31:46,000 We are beamed directly into people's brains. That is such a key thing. And they choose to listen to us, as well. I mean, I don't know about you, but I certainly have [BBC] Radio 4 on a lot when I'm around the house and it's quite a passive experience. I love Radio 4, don't get me wrong. But in many cases, listening to the radio is quite passive. But when I get my headphones on, you know that's it. I've chosen to have this medium delivered directly into my ears. And I think that's super powerful and something that – to say I find very moving is maybe a bit too much – but to think that people actually actively want that from us every week is really something, you know, and it makes me very, very proud that they choose to do that. And we know that people listen to it in their cars as well as when they're in the gym or cooking because they've told us that, you know, or in the lab, as [co-host] Nick [Howe] said. And so that, I think, is what this medium gives us. It's that super personalisation that maybe you wouldn't get if we were a radio show, for example.

Benjamin Thompson, The Nature Podcast

00:39:05,000 So when you get a senior scholar in this small room for an hour speaking only to you, even though they know that the recorder is running, even if the content is the same, the tenor is completely different, the mode of delivery is completely different [from the usual academic delivery].

Ian Pollock, The Familiar Strange

00:14:19,000 I would say it affords a strange opportunity for people to be a little bit more personal than they are in their regular academic work. And I take advantage of this, and I usually talk to people about it in the pre-interview, because some scholars aren't comfortable with it. But a lot of times when I'm talking to them about their project, I have the opportunity to ask them why it's personal to them. Like Thomas Laqueur, this great scholar. My favourite episode, I think, is *The Work of the Dead* – it's about the cultural history of what humans do with dead bodies. And he's kind of this secular Jewish guy, wouldn't consider himself to have any supernatural beliefs or anything like that, but toward the end of the episode, I got him talking about his dad who had died. His grandfather died in Germany during the [Second World] War and was buried there, and his dad fled. So, his dad and his grandfather were separated, and his wife convinced him to take the ashes of his dad back to Germany and bury them there with his grandfather.

So, he shared this very personal story that he mentions in the book – he mentions it in the book, it's how I knew about it – but hearing him really go into detail about it and hearing his voice and hearing him become emotional about it humanises the scholar and makes a connection, I think, with the listener that scholars are people, that they're not these abstract voices or distillers of knowledge. They have questions and doubts and interesting experiences, and the personal can really affect scholarship.

To hear people talk personally is something, I think, the podcast medium does better than any other medium, possibly even video, because there's even a little bit less self-consciousness when you're not on film. There's an intimacy to it that can really reach the personal side of scholarship and the personal investment and concerns and all of that stuff while also getting to the meat of what their scholarship says. It's not just all feelings and emotions and fun stuff, it's also got the academic stuff; it combines both of those things in ways that I don't see happening in other media.

Blair Hodges, The Maxwell Institute Podcast Podcast

00:02:19,000 I felt that a podcast about this topic matter would be an opportunity for me to explore something that was just fundamental about our practice as historians, but that we don't talk very much about, which is that obsession with archives, that love of that thrill of the chase, that hunt for that document, and the way that it makes us feel, the way our bodies feel when we're in that moment. I mean, you know, as academics, we do live so much in our heads. We talk about our ideas, but we don't talk about the ways that our bodies make us feel. But I knew that we all know that experience as historians, that we all have that in us. It's why generally most of us go through this slog of trying to get a job as an historian, whether as a professional or an academic historian, so that we can continue to research and go into the archives.

Clare Wright, Archive Fever

00:17:12,000 Because scholars are people and scholars know that, but they don't often talk about it. And people who are kind of just interested, you know, graduate-level type thinking people in the world who – maybe they're an accountant or, you know – they don't work in the academy. They don't get to experience those coffee chats. They don't get to sit down around a fire, drink a cup of coffee and talk to somebody about their research. All they see is this book that was produced, this thing of knowledge that's given to them. And so, it really can connect people with the human side of what scholarship is in ways that I don't think are accessible unless you have friends who are scholars or you're a scholar yourself. But even then, you don't get to experience it. If you're like an anthropologist, you might not get to experience it with a biologist.

Blair Hodges, The Maxwell Institute Podcast

00:53:07,000 When people talk about intimacy and podcasting, they're talking about relationships and they're describing these mediating relationships in terms of closeness, and that can be closeness through time or closeness through space. Thinking about touch, the idea that podcasts touch us in some way, or it can be closeness in terms of interaction, like how people interact with each other and how people interact with podcasts and how the hosts talk to each other and things like that. And these ways of describing intimacy aren't new; as long as there's been intimacy, there's been a negotiation of intimacy.

But what's happening is people are using these things that we've been talking about for a really, really long time, these negotiations we've had about what it means to be close to each other. And we're using it to describe those negotiations for podcasting. We're using these really old discussions to negotiate what it means to connect with each other through podcasting as a medium.

Alyn Euritt, podcast scholar

Vulnerable

When I first started podcasting, it was really hard to negotiate guest–interview–audience relationships to find a more intimate register. I was a PhD student at the time and was often interviewing academics much more senior than myself. But that was only part of it. It was also because I'd witnessed and experienced a fair amount of academic arseholeness in my time as an MA and a PhD student – destroying an argument rather than helping develop it, laughing at others for attempting to try something out of their comfort zone rather than acknowledging the attempt and helping find ways to make it work, or being snide rather than generous when offering critical feedback.

So I can understand why people don't like to open up when talking about their research. They've been conditioned to be guarded, to perform as the scholar who defends not discusses. Unsurprisingly, given academic cultures, I've made podcasts with people for whom intimacy was hard.

I've asked them questions and they've read back their pre-prepared answers, they've become tense if I start to ask about anything outside what they thought we'd speak about, or they've wanted to re-record themselves because they weren't happy with an expression or hesitation.

But scholarly podcasting can be, when done well, such a liberating experience. Intimacy opens the door to vulnerability. I think that to be comfortable with both one's own and others' sense of vulnerability is a way of developing processes of knowledge creation that are as dynamic and flexible as the things we scholars study (whatever they happen to be).

This means thinking about what happens when we bring together multiple, often divergent, voices into discussions, when there are moments of improvisation in what we produce, when the messiness of the method of inquiry is there for all to hear, and when we put 'unfinished' work with an unauthoritative tenor out there in the world.

Why does vulnerability seem so central to scholarly podcasting?

> 00:05:04,000 Vulnerability is really, really important in podcasting. And it's not surprising to me that other people have pointed to that and use that word. A lot of what I wrote in the intimacy chapter in *Podcasting: The Audio Media Revolution* had to do with trust. It had to do with a trust relationship that forms between listeners and podcast producers. And one of the arguments in that chapter is that the circuit of trust begins in the other direction. The circle of trust begins with the podcaster trusting the listener to approach the material that she or he is offering in a right way. That there is a kind of respect that is asked by the podcaster of the listener to treat the material as if it's between two friends and that vulnerability, that showing of yourself as fallible, as uncertain, as not authoritative, that speaking in a way that is so at odds with contemporary political discourse, which is about unmerited

confidence and braggadocio, that's the opposite register of podcasting. So, this vulnerability that other people are pointing to in and around podcasting is a really important part of that intimate relationship. You can't have an intimate relationship without some sense of vulnerability, both on the part of the podcaster and on the part of the listener.

… We [academics] were trained to know where you're going before you take your first step and to construct an argument, have a hypothesis, and test it. And then once you've found your result, you organise all of your words to arrive at that destination. And that's not the way podcasts seem to work. And I can understand why conventional, more older-school academics might be a little bit troubled by that. And, you know, for centuries, academics have been viewed as kind of the font of definitive knowledge in a lot of ways. And podcasting is not that. But the argument is, my argument is, that academia doesn't need to be that either. And it can be a richer, more discursive, more dialogic, more speculative, more conversational experience than it has been throughout most of my professional life and throughout the past several centuries of higher learning.

Martin Spinelli, podcast scholar

00:22:34,000 The idea already written in the idea of the written text is you have to give the shortest way, spare me the rest. Spare me the tedious work you had to do to come up with this. It doesn't matter because now I have the shortcut so I can prove it. And the shortcut means I have to put arguments together to show you that according to this theory and that methodology and those data and these subjects I can get to that conclusion, and this is my result now. But I doubt that this is really true. I seriously doubt it. It is against every one of my experiences of doing research.

Moritz Klenk, Podlog

00:24:42,000 And another thing about math – this is especially true of academic math papers – is when you see the finished product, all of the gory, gritty, false steps and all that was taken out of it... Our discipline is based on this idea of truth, right? These things are logically true. And we obscure in that process the stacks and stacks and stacks of scrap paper that you used to get where you were going. And so, it's nice to hear people talk about mathematics because you're not obscuring the scrap paper.

Kevin Knudson, My Favorite Theorem

00:12:03,000 Like a lot of people, I had a pretty tough grad school experience, and I was very, very nervous about putting my voice out there and being piled on for being wrong. I just was not super comfortable. I think one thing I've had to deal with, and a lot of people deal with in academia, is my personal style is not the assertion of my original idea and then, like, 'boom, there it is. Everyone deal with it'. I much prefer to be in conversation with others and develop ideas together. And so podcasting was a great medium for being part of a bigger conversation, but doing it in a way that felt more connected to the modes of communication I'm comfortable with and I enjoy. And that meant often just talking to a friend, a smart friend, about a subject that I thought was important and interesting.

Then it's discursive, right? I can change my mind during the course of the podcast because [co-host] Noorain [Khan] says something that convinces me and vice versa. Whereas in writing, for the most part, particularly single-authored work and particularly academic work, it's about advancing an argument. I mean, the word argument: 'right here is my claim. Here is my argument. I'm putting it out there now'. You can attack it if you want to. You can engage with it, which, you know, sometimes people do without attacking as well, which is nice. But it's much more declarative than it is discursive, usually. And it takes a long time for it to become more of a conversation. Whereas in podcasting, you can do that conversation in real time… and it was, in a way, something that Noorain and I had done for years before that already. So, it was very natural for us and helpful for me to remember that as I was making my way through academia; that academia doesn't have to always be the way it's always been. And in trying other mediums and models of ways of thinking through ideas, maybe you can change it too.

Maria Sachiko Cecire, In Theory

00:43:56,000 I think it's an emergent thing. It feels like a process of drafting. You know, it has good bits, it has funny bits, bits I'm quite proud of or whatever, but it isn't finished. It's like handing in your PhD draft and going, 'that's it', when actually it's still a mess of chapters just loosely tied together. When you're writing something for a publication it's almost always the last bit where the magic happens, where it all comes together, where it becomes a complete thing in itself. And my sense is that that's what's missing.

Philip Roscoe, How to Build a Stock Exchange:
Making Finance Fit for the Future

00:56:57,000 But I think an interesting conversation maybe to have down the road is scholars who have gotten into podcasting, how podcasting has transformed their writing practice. Because I also really write differently, and I also find myself wanting to write more like I talk. And that includes writing shorter chapters, trying to move away from this desperate desire to make everything watertight and inarguable and to leave more openings and more possibilities for conversation. Because I think so much more now about how to actually engage people rather than, 'how do I create an impenetrable sphere of argument'.

Hannah McGregor, Secret Feminist Agenda
and podcast scholar

00:15:27,000 Why do you need to be authoritative? I think you definitely have to be rigorous and all of the rules that apply to writing a research paper or conducting research apply for podcasting as well. You need to be thorough and accurate in your research and you have to be honest in what you're writing, but I think podcasting allows you to be more honest about the fact that you're a person behind those results. And I think there is a certain dishonesty in academic writing, because you have this role as a professor or as whatever your function is at the point when you're writing a paper, and it's hiding the fact that you're a human being and you might make mistakes, might not be sure about what you're writing or what you're producing. While in podcasting, because you hear a human voice and because you hear the hesitations or hear the questions or the certainty you can transmit emotions...

If the whole field of academia is constructed in such a way that you have to sound authoritative and you have to sound final and definite it creates this hostile environment where everybody's in competition and everybody has to be right. And I think people are performing these roles a lot in writing. You have a voice in writing as well, and if it's expected of you to have this type of voice and to say things in these very definite ways, I think it creates an environment where people who are more insecure or people who have less of an ego find it very difficult to penetrate or to succeed in this environment. Maybe shaking that up a bit and allowing voices that sound authoritative in writing to speak in a less authoritative way is a good thing.

Dumitriţa Holdiş, Down, but Not Out

Pedagogical

Whenever I can, I bring podcasting into my teaching. It's a way of importing the intimacy and vulnerability of the form into the classroom. Other teachers have put their lectures online for their students or created repositories of conversations on given topics (whilst despairing at alienating interfaces, which feel anything but intimate). Teaching through podcasting doesn't stop at faculty-produced content, of course. Students can create podcast course assignments, and though this requires some class time given over to the craft, in my and others' experiences students embrace the chance to showcase and develop skills beyond writing and, when possible, jump at the opportunity to create public scholarship (and indeed often take it much more seriously than some do with essays).

How have university teachers used podcasting?

00:04:44,000 And then finally in '06, I guess it was around this time, I sent an email to the Academic Dean and I said, 'I'm going to record my lectures and put them on the open Internet'. I didn't say, 'can I?' I said, 'this is what I'm going to do' because it's my intellectual property. It actually says that in our collective agreement. Because we have a union, and it's a pretty strong union. So, he said 'this sounds like a great idea'. So, I did that. And then I got to the point, now, I actually record now on my phone because there's apps you can use... it got to the point where it's basically second nature. The students all know they're being recorded. So that's no big deal. And the student grades went up about six percent comparing before I started and after with the same classes and the same evaluations. So, either I got really good or my students got really good or it was probably the podcasts. So that's probably what it was.

My guess is that it's because you can go back and listen to stuff, because it hasn't affected my attendance. It just doesn't. I usually teach upper year classes. My department, I think, doesn't let me teach Intro because I think I scare students. I teach upper year things where people want to be in those classes anyway, or they have to be. No one wants to be in advanced univariate statistics.

Nobody. But they have to for their honour's degree, so they take it right. So people want to be in the class. So it's not the attendance it's the fact they can go back and listen to something.

It's easy for me to say to people when they come to my office and say, 'there's something I didn't understand in class today'. And I say, 'let's just go back and listen to it. What? Oh, that stuff. OK. Let's listen here now. Now, tell me what you understand about that'. Because it might be that I said it poorly. So at least I can listen to it. It helps me do my job better. But I think also it's a great studying tool. I mean, I can take a look at my site traffic before tests and exams, and it goes up 70–100 percent. Because they're just listening, listening, listening. So, I think it's useful for that. I think it also, in a completely self-serving way, it helps me do things better because I actually know what I said last time I thought something.

00:09:45,000 I swear a lot, like I don't swear badly in class. I don't say motherfucker or anything like that. But if something's bullshit, I just say it's bullshit. Like, 'oh, that's a bullshit idea'. Something like that. If I'm talking about Freud, I call him a dirty old man, and say it's bullshit. At first, I thought, 'I can't do that'. Then I thought, 'wait a second, that's who you are. Just do that…' I will make jokes to the class, 'oh I'll edit that out' and I've edited it I think maybe three times and there's 1300 classes posted and I think I've edited out three things. And they were usually things students said. Like a student said something and it's like 'you don't want that in the open internet, buddy. You just admitted that you're on acid'.

Dave Brodbeck, Spit and Twitches & creates podcasts from lectures

00:05:23,000 The idea is to try to create a repository of podcasts that can keep up with an International Development intro course in a changing world. So, I will try to do probably between three or four seasons a year, and ten podcasts each on average. So, you're looking at maybe 40 a year that will come out. And from there, I can pick and choose what works best for whoever.

There's two sections of the class that include ten modules each. So, in the class, the podcasts are stacked in this way. There's what they call a core. And that's very didactic, that's me lecturing to you, and there's visuals, we're clarifying points, I'm telling stories, we're sharing anecdotes. That's the basis of whatever the topic is – it's neoliberalism, it's globalisation, it's colonialism, whatever. Those all stay locked behind the university firewall. So those do not get released. They comprise the core content of the class. It's not visible in the public format.

In the class itself the podcasts are categorised in two areas. One's called Expert Analysis, and one's called Development in Action. Expert Analysis is where I find someone who's able to speak as an expert to the theme of that week. So, if we're talking about colonialism, as opposed to just sitting down and look-ing at the bullet points or, you know, reinterpreting Edward Said or others, I'll find someone who can dis-cuss colonialism with me over a 30-minute chat. And then the second one is called Development in Action, where we feature someone who's doing active research and development. The Expert Analysis is key because if you've got a lot of students who are foreign to Can-ada and English is not their first language, they may not grapple with what colonialism or neoliberalism or other sort of jargoned word is just by bullet points. Rather, they can get a deeper sense of it through con-versational association. So, you and I sitting down for a half hour and just chatting about it is effectively a really important tool for English as a second language learners.

00:45:33,000 One of the things that I feel is a challenge with distance learning is those really busy interfaces, the really busy platforms. I don't think that it produces a sense of community, the sense to commune. I think it presents a show where you are just watching a guy and a bunch of technology go across your screen. And I think that within the search for any knowledge and experience of university, people do want a sense of community. And my question going forward would be, is radio, podcasting, audio, is that experience in itself an ability to create that sense of a cohort and community? Because with Corona, you've got the brick-and-mortar universities around the world going online, and you bet that the administrators are going to be saying, 'why do we have this expensive real estate?' Well, the reason for that is because the university experience just isn't always a class. It is a sense of community that comes out of it. My question is, would podcasting further or limit it?

Robert Huish, Global Development Primer

00:15:16,000 So it's so awesome to do a podcast, but the biggest challenge I found was balancing it with everything else. And you really just have to say, 'screw it' to everything else and just spend that time preparing and reading. And it's fun, though, because I think the biggest benefit for me was being forced to read books I normally wouldn't read. Or books that I'm interested in, but I just wouldn't read, and then to have the interview with the author. I just learn so much. Or with like a key policymaker. Like I learn so much from that. And I still just use those podcasts in my classrooms, and it just simply reinforces what I'm actually teaching in the class, in the classroom. And then the students can see that I'm not just this professor that teaches theoretically or from the book or something, but I actually know what I'm talking about and I know the state of the world or the state of the field. And by having the experts talk, just as a guest speaker would, in the podcast format, it demonstrates that you're at the leading edge of your field, I think. Even if you don't have the academic publication in that area.

Michael LaBelle, Energy and Innovation

00:02:21,000 I teach a course called Environmental Communication that I've taught for 12 years. It used to be a traditional seminar, then I turned it into an undergraduate class that was fairly large. At a certain point I realised that probably the next step in the evolution for that course was to get out of the classroom. Through the Provost at the University Minnesota I was able to get a grant as part of its Learning Innovations programme, which is really nice. It was a great opportunity to actually get support and rationalisation and legitimation for doing this. So, I called it a 'digitally networked field course'. The idea is to get students out of the classroom into the field sites where they are going to state parks etc. We're in the middle of an urban area, so it's pretty easy for them with public transportation, to get to these state parks...

I started in 2017, that's four years ago. For the most part, it was a means for me to deliver information to them. It was an informal thing where I'd interview some people and I'd go out to parks and say, 'and the next step for your assignment is this'. It started kind of converging at that point. And frankly, the convergence never really was consummated for years, especially because I teach the class usually about once a year as opposed to two semesters. So, there was all that other time. It was dead space for the podcast.

So last year I had a research sabbatical, and I decided every week starting on Earth Day – and now I've done it every week since last Earth Day – I would do one of these and really start building it up and then gift it over, if you will. I'd stay the executive producer, but my associate producer is now a student. And now all the content is being produced by students. So, it really is a matter of me kind of now having done this and built it a little bit, getting out of the way, and having students produce content.

Mark Pedelty, Public Lands Podcast

00:08:20,000 For me, I have to start at the very beginning. And that's why I say I start with a template. I tell the students, 'all you have to do is show up with your voice and a little bit of research'. I have a very structured first assignment where I put them in groups of three and they do a roundtable discussion, and that's it. And I give them the topic and I give them a script, it's a scripted opening and then they get to talk about whatever they want to talk about. Let's say it's art and entertainment, they will have done their research on three or four arts and entertainment stories. It has to be local, regional, and international. And then they'll have a dialogue. There'll be a host and the host will introduce the topics and the other two will jump in and they'll have a discussion. And it's supposed to be an organic conversation. So that's one way. That's to get them comfortable in the studio and comfortable with their colleagues and comfortable with their own voices. And then we do baby steps from there. To move on to doing interviews, to writing scripts, to gathering that sound. Of course, all the other editing that goes with that, finding music, building the narrative. And we manage to get it done in 12 to 15 weeks.

Kim Fox, podcast scholar

00:11:34,000 One of the things that we [Kimberley Moore, Janis Thiessen and I] wanted to do with this [Manitoba Food History] project, that I think might stand out that's a little different than some of the other academic podcasts, is we were heavily influenced by the curated works of Charles Hardy III, who is in West Chester University. He does oral history. His background is in radio journalism, but he's done a lot of experimental radio plays and stuff like, well, radio pieces, I don't know how to explain it. But he takes oral histories and makes really amazing sound art out of them. But one of the things he does is he integrates good oral history and digital scholarship into his class and he's teaching students how to do sound mapping and podcasting and all sorts of other facets to up their skill set. A lot of the students in the United States and some of the universities will have a digital portfolio that includes how to create podcasts. One of the things that we really wanted to do was make sure that we could teach podcasting as part of the classes that we're engaged in and utilise this project as a way to allow these students to actually produce something of note that they could do publicly as a form of public scholarship.

…It's a different process than writing your typical essay, but I feel it's similar in a lot of ways. We teach audio storytelling in class and how to convert your typical essay into a podcast script. And what we discovered is we get the same amount of drops that you would for any course, but the amount of research that students do for the project, because it will be a form of public performance – they have to narrate their project, edit it – they'll exceed what they would normally do with a typical essay. They'll find different sources and dig into archives and find secondary sources and just draw stories out of the original source material or the interviews.

Kent Davies, Preserves and podcast instructor

00:17:21,000 It really was very student driven. I had the idea to focus on vultures, but really the work that emerged, we really co-learnt together. I think something like podcasts really do require a team, and then it's such a great avenue for students to learn everything from script writing to the research they need to go into it, then all the audio skills that you need to edit. I've loved working with our team because everybody brings different skill sets.

Krista Caballero, EH Out Loud

00:05:00,000 And so I taught the class in 2012, I thought ok, this is the podcast I've been waiting to do. So way back in 2008, when I said at some point I'm going to do the podcast I want to do, but I need to learn how to do podcasts, that came in 2012. And what I did is I got a group of graduate students in Public History and New Media. And I turned them on to the *History of the World in 100 Objects*, which I think was one of the first podcasts I listened to. Not the first, but one of the first. And I said, 'look, we could take this model of looking at objects and creating this material culture as history, but do it for Central Florida, like we have all these museums, and they have all these objects, and they tell these stories. So let's use this History of the World... but do it for Central Florida', and so that's what the class did.

And I controlled the production, I made sure that all of the recordings were equal as far as the quality of recording. We all workshopped all the scripts and we all worked together. It's only a 16-week semester, so at the end we had essentially a blueprint of how the project would work. And I had, I think, nine students in the class. And at the end of the semester, I said, 'look, you all have given me a plan for how to produce this podcast. If you want to volunteer and produce this podcast, we'll figure out a way to get a production schedule and a production flow going. You don't have to do this. I'll do it myself'.

And every student in the class volunteered. And over the course of two and a half years, we produced this History of Central Florida podcast. I think out of all the podcasts I've produced, it's probably the most important one and the one that's got the most traction and attention.

Robert Cassanello, History of Central Florida

Transformative

Freeing

I like writing journal articles, and all the stuff that goes around them, but I don't write many of them. Come to think of it, maybe that's why I like writing them? When I write them, I do my best impression of being authoritative and produce conclusion-orientated, heavily-referenced pieces. Before writing them, I present them at conferences or, if I'm lucky, at invited talks. After submitting them, the reviewers typically ask for a lot more references from authors who are usually already cited a lot, and also provide occasionally really brilliantly useful and sometimes difficult to comprehend comments. Some people read these articles, and every now and again people engage with them.

And that's all great. There's a lot to be said for scientific writing having a certain recognisable format and generic conventions because it can ease communication between our peers, but if that were my sole means of intellectual expression I don't think I'd stay in academia. Students are great, but the publication treadmill is sometimes so idiotic that I'm embarrassed to explain it to my friends outside academia:

Yeah, I spent 2 years doing fieldwork in India, then had no space to write about it properly in the article I produced because I had to fill it up with references by people at British universities. Oh and it took 2 years to get published and 6 people have cited it, but it's still considered a 'good thing' to have done because it's in a 'high-ranked' journal. Nah. No thanks.

Podcasting, for me, has been a process of intellectual free-ing. And the freeing is something worth constantly fighting for so that we are worth more than our publication count; because it can often seem as if no one cares about what's actually in standard academic outputs in any case; so we can find time for joyful, generative work that pushes the boundaries of what's considered scholarship; and so that we can build our own projects whilst also spreading a healthy dose of careful uncertainty across academia at large. And wouldn't it be wonderful if we could do more of academia like that.

What can podcasting do for academia?

> 00:00:47,000 I think it can, I'm hoping it can, drive a wedge into the door of the ivory tower and help pry it open for people who are not so amenable to the hegemony of the written word. I want a little medal for working the word hegemony in there. I mean, in academia, there's certain expectations. For example, I remember when I was first asked to write up my CV in a given format, it was a format that was required by a funding body and the format required that the very first thing on your CV underneath your name was a number. And that number was meant to be how many publications you have. And they didn't want the names. I mean, probably there was a space for it later in the CV, but they wanted a number front and centre. And I felt like I was no longer a human being, that I just needed to have this number tattooed on my head and that obviously the higher the number, the better a scholar you were supposedly. Right. But, you know, this was early in my career. And I mean, I'm mid-career now and I still don't have a lot of publications under my belt because my M.O. has been to try to dis-seminate what I'm working on in alternate formats. I will do interactive sound installations or I will hack a physical object to become an interactive object, to play with data and kind of understand some of the data

that I've collected. So that number for me was meaningless and totally dehumanising. And so, I think what podcasts can do for academia is help humanise it.

Lori Beckstead, podcast scholar

00:30:12,000 I don't feel like it's changed my scholarly identity, but I feel like it's changed my scholarly habitus. That's a jargony term from Pierre Bourdieu meaning how one is predisposed to operate in the world essentially. Podcasting gave us an appetite and the courage to start experimenting more with the forms of scholarly communication. I don't think we would have ended up putting a plaque on a mountain to honour a dead glacier had we not started podcasting and realised there was something really rewarding about being multimodal, having a multiple approach to the forms of scholarly communication and being open to para-scholarly kinds of output. So, I think it's a big confidence builder in a sense.

We all know how to write a research article at this point in our career. We also know how many people read those articles, typically. You can invest your time and energy in trying to write the perfect article that is published at the perfect time and gets a huge resonance but it's often like trying to find a diamond in a mine. Or you can try to take a broader approach and say, 'OK, we've got something we want to say. Let's spread it across a number of different media and events and practices and see if we can multiply the impact that way'. I think that podcasting started us on that path. More of a change in practice than a change in identity.

Dominic Boyer, Cultures of Energy

00:10:02,000 It's taken years and years to realise no one at the university really cares what I do. No one cares what I write. I mean, no, but it's true. Wait, I don't know if I should say that... actually no one is gonna read it in this book anyway. Honestly, like no one. I mean, in the department, no one cares what I do. I just published something, you know? Like no one cares. No one fucking cares! And it was bothering me for two years or so. And then now I'm like, 'what, what is my problem? I can do whatever I want!' And so, I finished the book. Now I do whatever I want. Sure, I'll do more publications, but I'm going to have fun. I'm gonna do other stuff on the Internet now. Like no one cares. Like to be internationally kind of competitive or normal. Yeah. Two publications a year, work with some students, too. Because I don't have that many years of experience and I really struggle to write journal articles, like it's a real struggle. It's really a lot of work. But the podcast is like, let me have some fun.

Michael LaBelle, Energy and Innovation

00:45:00,000 It's encouraged me to be even more free-form about what I do than I already was. I mean, I'll confess that I was never the most orthodox scholar [laughs] but it's definitely encouraged me to think about ways that I can make things even wackier. And it's definitely been good in the sense that, ironically, the school is always like, 'oh, what you need to do is have a national profile and blah, blah, blah'. I'm like, 'well, motherfucker, here you go: national profile [laughs]. Take it or leave it. How'd you like them apples? [laughs]'

Brian L. Frye, Ipse Dixit

00:17:26,000 You have to find the time, like these little nuggets of time interspersed within everything else that you have to do. You'll have this schedule, like, man, we've been trying for so long to have a schedule so we have an episode every month. It never happens because something always comes up that we have to do before we can do the podcasting. So, it's created kind of an outside podcaster identity where I go in and I'm like, 'I'm doing these things on the periphery of my work that probably most people in my department don't even notice'. And it kind of helps me. It's kind of a therapy for the work.

00:23:41,000 There's a real sort of generative nature of us doing the podcasting that's outside of our traditional academic work. And I think there is a lot of intellectual freedom there for sure, and artistic freedom.

Samuel M. Clevenger, Somatic Podcast

00:27:17,000 I said right at the beginning the reason that I wanted to do this was because I thought it would be fun. And I still find it fun. We have a lot of fun working together and we enjoy this process very much and one of the things that is so enjoyable about it is that it's collaborative… and humanities scholars tend to work in isolation. And so, all of this stuff goes on in our heads all of the time. And what is so lovely about making this podcast is that it's a social object that we're creating and we're creating together. And I feel like [co-host] Yves [Rees] and I learn from each other so much of the time and at the same time as we are learning from the people that we are interviewing. It becomes this kind of very beautiful circle of life.

Clare Wright, Archive Fever

To build on what [co-host] Clare [Wright] was saying about it being fun and about it being collaborative and about it being embodied. They're all things I really value about the podcast as well. And I've come to really think about that mode of knowledge production as a feminist intervention. The kind of masculinist norms of the academy values, you know, solitary, disembodied, serious, earnest, rational scholarship, it valorises that as the only way to produce knowledge and be an intellectual. And so, to be engaged in really serious ideas and at the same time laughing and really enjoying yourself feels actually like a really deeply political thing to be doing.

Yves Rees, Archive Fever

Oh, my God, you've just articulated that so well. I've just always thought of that as being a bit of a 'fuck you' to the academy, but you've put really nice words to it.

Clare Wright, Archive Fever

00:11:46,000 I define legal scholarship as broadly as I can. So, amongst other things, one of the correspondents for the podcast is an incarcerated person who goes by the pseudonym King. I've interviewed him on a stolen cell phone several times in prison. And he's also sent me podcast episodes via WhatsApp that I can use that he records with people inside the prison. For me, it's really just a way of thinking outside the box in terms of what we're doing when we do legal scholarship and thinking more broadly about the context in which we think about ideas and ideas about the law.

Brian L. Frye, Ipse Dixit

00:01:03,000 The audio media revolution is podcasting full stop. Not since radio in the early 20th century have we seen such a change in the way people are listening and the way people are making sense out of what they're hearing. It has its own semantic register. It has its own aesthetic dimension. It has its own characteristics which are completely unique to it and different from radio. That's my argument.

One of the things that is offered by podcasting that will have an effect on academia and that will, and perhaps should, affect the way academics do their work is that the podcasting register is necessarily more intimate and more conversational than previous audio media and much more intimate and conversational than conventional lectures and certainly 99 percent of academic writing. And what that brings with it is a kind of contingency and a kind of discursivity and a kind of open-endedness that is much more about different frameworks for a particular problem or a particular issue than it is about coming up with information or data or resolving something or landing at a truth with a capital T. So all of those things that are the traditional domain of academics – authority and certainty and building a case for something based on stacks of evidence, all of those things are undermined by the way podcasting exists and podcasting happens. And academics, who are bright and clever and very interesting people, can really, should really, not be anxious about the postmodern nature of podcasting and the way it undermines, or forces us to rethink, certain conventional ideas of knowledge and conventional ideas of learning.

Martin Spinelli, podcast scholar

Upskilling

Last night a podcast changed my life. And the day before. And last Tuesday morning. Podcasting changes me because making podcasts regularly is an ongoing, amazing upskilling exercise. It has pushed me to think about scientific communication in different ways and doing loads and loads of podcasts has also, I hope, made me read better, listen better, and talk better.

How has podcasting changed other scholars' working lives?

> 00:13:21,000 I would say it's definitely made me smarter, for sure. That is without a doubt. And honestly that is one of the motivating factors because I learn so much. It can be in an area that I am an expert in, but I'm still finding, 'oh I found this new study', or 'there's this new detail I wasn't aware of.' So, it has impacted my outlook, I would say. I always have a bigger picture now when I approach science. I feel like I always have, but one thing that I've realised in my department, and in neuroscience, is sometimes the bigger picture or focussing upon the patient can be lost in regard to the goal

of the research. And doing this podcast and remaining connected with the community has helped me to keep that, to help keep the patient in mind and realise that that is why I'm doing my research. So, it's given me a new perspective.

Stephanie Caligiuri, The People's Scientist

00:15:54,000 I think that doing podcasting, especially for so long, has made me a better conversationalist. I can sit down now with anybody, not even know anything about them and have a conversation easily. You know, it's all about asking questions and listening to them. You know, you have to listen! I really don't like when people interview me and they have 10 questions and they just ask them one by one. They don't go back and forth. I think that's the beauty of the podcast. You have to listen to people. I will often have a list of questions and mostly I don't go to them. I have the first one and I just listen and then it all pops into my head. So, I think that's helped my academic pursuits enormously. It's made me a better teacher, it's made me a better scientist, because I now read papers in many different fields and that informs our own work. So, I look at this as career development. I think it's been terrific.

00:22:33,000 I've learnt to be a great conversationalist totally from podcasts. It drives my wife nuts. She said, 'everything with you is a question now. All you do is ask questions'. Isn't that what a conversation is about? And she doesn't like it at all. If I start asking questions, she'll leave [laughs].

Vincent Racaniello, This Week in Virology

00:26:36,000 Well, very, very quickly, after we started podcasting, I realised that one of the other things that it was doing, and it probably doesn't sound like it now because I'm just rabbiting on, was it really helped me to understand how much we could fit into 20 minutes. To think about, 'okay, there is somebody sitting on the other end of this, who has to listen to this'. So, in a strange way, it improved my ability to talk to time. And it also helped me with writing as well, not just from the point of view of analysis, but being able to realise that sometimes when we're trying to force the academic prose, actually, we probably, want to go back to how we would explain it if we were speaking to somebody. And for me, it has been really, hugely helpful for my other academic work, in the production of other academic papers... I think part of that probably comes down to the fact that people don't talk about their writing practices very often. And I think, for me, it became very clear that talking through the podcast just translated into much more confident writing practices where I'm not trying to tie myself in knots about ideas.

Michaela Benson, Brexit Brits Abroad

00:08:59,000 I know now I've got this thing where I start a sentence and then I qualify it, and then I go back to finishing the sentence all the time, and it really annoys me. I actually now make a conscious decision that I just go through the sentence right to the end, as much as possible, rather than making numerous qualifications in one entire sentence because it doesn't actually help in terms of a flow of a train of thought or a concept or an argument or whatever. And I think it's made me a better communicator just to learn how to do this.

**Dario Llinares, The Cinematologists and
podcast scholar**

00:22:28,000 I think there's another point, which is academic solitude. I think there's something to be said about producing knowledge together via these routes of writing and reviewing and approval or academic connection or academic networking, which more often than not really does bring out so much insecurity and so much hiding behind titles and positions and precarity. And I think that [podcasting] also does something to the sociality of being in academia together and creating knowledge together. So, I think this act of just having a conversation, but not having a debate, just having a conversation where we build things together, again adds to the industry in ways that are not present in the current formats.

Corina Enache, The Human Show

00:28:22,000 We had a conversation last night with a kind of a legendary filmmaker, probably the most legendary filmmaker we've had on. And then this morning, we had a conversation with two colleagues about teaching film in 2020. And both those conversations made me excited to work, to plan my teaching and to do the podcast and share those conversations with people and just do the work. And that's, I guess, what I get from podcasting, which is what is definitely missing on a day-to-day basis. It's no fault of my colleagues or students, it's not about apportioning blame, it's about the realities of working in higher education. And we've carved out a space where we can embrace that aspect of it. And I know that I get a lot from that, and I feel like, 'yeah, I'm doing good work' because these conversations are making me think about, okay, 'what am I gonna do tomorrow, and how can I do it differently?' and bringing those people's experiences into my work, I think is really valuable.

Neil Fox, The Cinematologists and podcast scholar

00:31:15,000 It's almost a running joke in the legal academy that when people give a paper presentation, you'll have some dude, always a dude in the audience, who says, 'well, I didn't read your paper, but I have a question that's more of a comment. And let me tell you about my work' [laughs] Right? Right? I mean, that's like the model of the academic 'conversation'. One of the things that I really wanted to do was not to be like that. One of the big commitments I made with the podcast was every interview I do, I read the whole paper or the whole book before I do the podcast. And I think about it. And I write down the questions that I think somebody who wants to learn about this person's ideas would want to know the answers to, based on what I thought after reading the paper. And then when I do the interview, I just listen. Right. I mean, like, you know, I've got questions, but the questions aren't as important as listening to what the other person has to say and trying to understand what they think is important. And I really see that as being the primary goal. But, you know, I mean, as scholars, I think one thing that, unlike yourself, most scholars are not good at doing is listening to what other people have to say and actually paying attention to what they say.

Brian L. Frye, Ipse Dixit

Rewarding

If I'm going to be completely honest with you, I had no idea about what an academic career was meant to look like. I have an aunt with a PhD in geology who makes a living as a tour guide and a great-uncle who edited an encyclopaedia and wrote books on politics. I never really thought about life after a PhD before embarking on one in 2009, but getting paid to research and write seemed like a good way to spend half a decade. And it was (for the most part).

But then you're done, or you're almost done, and lots of well-meaning senior people give you advice – usually along the lines of 'publish in certain journals to get certain jobs in certain places'. And it sort of stressed me out for a bit. It seemed like a very narrow way of conceiving an intellectual life, and I wasn't really overconcerned about the search for prestige or validation that preoccupies many academics.

So I was happy to find that scholarly podcasting, which I found rewarding, can be both work in and around 'mainstream academia' and also 'serious scholarly work' that translates into paid jobs or promotions as more and more university departments are recognising its value (which may or may not kill podcasting's vitality). But aside from this, podcasting can help careers by giving younger scholars an excuse to talk to people or as a way of raising their profile or getting recognition.

In what ways has scholarly podcasting changed the ways in which scholarly work is rewarded?

00:22:45,000 Podcasting has changed my view of what constitutes a publication. When I came out of grad school, which was like 1993, it's quite a while ago. When I came out of grad school, and I came out of a very prestigious programme, the most cited psychology programme in the world... And you know, so I came out of this thinking anything that someone does that isn't in a high-end journal is garbage because I was 27 and an idiot. So, you know, we all are at that age. What happened was it changed the way I think of this, because I know that I'm reaching more people with even my lectures or with *Spit and Twitches* or the other stuff that I do. I know I'm reaching more people than I do if I write an article. I guarantee that. I mean, I've written some good stuff, like I'm not a complete loser, but I think it has more impact on my field than an article I write. And that really surprises me. I still publish things and it's important that I do that, and I do it because I want to. But when I write something now, I think to myself, I wonder how many people actually read this... So on the other hand, I can put one of these episodes out of *Spit and Twitches* and be blown away by the fact that thousands of people have listened to me talk with my friend Chris about birdsong and the neural basis of it. And it's like, 'how is this happening?' So that kind of thing. So, yeah, it's changed that for sure. And I have now a better view of that kind of work than I used to. Because I'm a somewhat senior person here, a lot of times I'm asked to write letters of recommendation for people that are up for tenure, up for promotion, and when I do that, when I look at their CV, it used to be I'd look at someone's CV and if it had a bunch of things that were not in *Science* or *Nature*, I'd be like 'loser'. I'm not like that anymore. It's more like, 'oh, that takes work and it's valuable and it's good'.

Dave Brodbeck, Spit and Twitches & lecture podcasts

00:18:08,000 I have done a lot of navigating and thinking in the Australian context. We have this issue, it's known as the idea of tall poppies, which I found less of when I was in the UK, and the metaphor of the tall poppy is that Australians don't like people that get a bit too fancy or stick their neck out or kind of go above and beyond. I feel like there was a little bit of that early on. It's always hard to know how much of that is other people, or just your own weird sub-genre of imposter syndrome. That people think that you are being fancier somehow than them or you're showing them up in some strange way. So, yeah, I've spent a bit of time thinking about it from that perspective. I spent a lot of time thinking about it in terms of the narrative of my academic identity and academic productivity as well.

There is definitely this sense in academia that if you're a mid-stage to a late-stage PhD, you're just finding your feet, whereas, in any other industry, if you'd been actively working in that industry for four or five years, you wouldn't be considered so junior. I very deliberately recently, like in the last two years, started rebranding myself as a mid-career researcher because you realise you can just get stuck in this idea that you're an early career researcher for over a decade and it's kind of absurd in any other industry. And so, I think that plays into it a lot. This idea of when you have the authority to speak on behalf of your discipline.

Lauren Gawne, Lingthusiasm

36:23,000 What I'm really realising now, as a tenure track faculty member who is increasingly on tenure and promotion committees myself, is that, you're right, it's a managerial stance, but for the most part, at least in Canada, it does not come from high-level administrators, this conservatism around what constitutes the scholarly, it comes from the people sitting on tenure and promotion committees. It comes from your colleague down the hall who has always done everything in an incredibly conventional and conservative fashion and can only recognise things that look like what they've done as real scholarship and are going to absolutely hold everybody to that standard if it's the last thing they do. A colleague of mine referred to it as the 'frozen middle' in the university, that it's like, it's not a top and it's not the bottom, it's this weird stuck portion in the middle and it's that middle that tends to be on tenure and promotion committees.

I got pushback from all sides. The people who think that real scholarly podcasting has to be that highly produced, highly aesthetic, you know, NPR style audio storytelling, and so look at an interview podcast and are like, 'well, that's nothing. Anybody can do an interview'. I get disdain from them. I get disdain from people in the podcasting world who are like, 'why would anybody care about scholarship? What a boring podcast'. I get disdain from academics who are like, 'OK, well, that's cute, but you still have to do the real work'. Like, you know, every field has its gatekeepers. Wherever you look, you're going to find people who are invested in making everything look the same or invested in getting to control what things look like or what things sound like. But I have also found that the further I get into my career, I find it easier and easier to ignore them, because they're so boring. When people tell you that you're not allowed to do a thing, it's wildly boring, they're wildly boring people. So instead, you go and find the people who are excited and interested in the idea of doing things differently, because there's tonnes of them too it turns out.

Hannah McGregor, Secret Feminist Agenda
and podcast scholar

00:57:02,000 There's, of course, a bigger issue in academia these days of how to give professional credit for non-traditional work like podcasting. Like you're coming up for tenure and you have a successful podcast. How should that be counted? And there is no clear answer to any of this. If you write op-eds for the newspaper, that's hugely important, but might not count as traditional scholarship. So podcasting falls into that same kind of category. Academia needs to figure out what kind of thing podcasting is and what kind of credit you should get for doing it. And nobody's figured it out yet. And one of the nice things, I'm a full professor, so I don't need to worry about these questions. But I should say I would not have done this ten years ago. That would have been a really bad idea for my career. So, it would be nice if we could make an academic environment in which people were encouraged to do this kind of work instead of discouraged from it.

Matt Stanley, What the If?

00:12:09,000 The institutional support came later. I was working part time, not having a stable job, at the University of Pittsburgh's Russia Centre. I was basically a temp worker. And at some point they have to make a decision to cut you loose or keep you on. I approached them, I said, 'hey, look, you know, I could basically offer you the podcast'. And that evolved into now developing and integrating the Centre's programming into the podcast...

01:03:52,000 Once I had an academic tell me to stop blogging and it's like, well, 'fuck you, if I stopped blogging, I wouldn't have a fucking job right now' because I didn't get an academic job. I didn't get a faculty tenure track faculty job. And thank God I did the blog and I turned it into this podcast because who knows where I'd be today. Probably far less happier than I am now. I mean, I love what I'm doing and I'm grateful for the opportunity to do it. But academia didn't save me. I saved myself [laughing].

Sean Guillory, SRB Podcast

00:23:27,000 Obviously, I had a choice to make and I got to the end of my career, my training student career, and I had PhD and a medical degree. I had the top results in my year, and I had all the year prizes and I could have become a medical superstar. I could have probably carried on doing a lot of good science and maybe been a science superstar, or I could have gone into communications, and I knew if I went into communicating things, I would have to be a superstar because otherwise I'd be letting the side down...

... And there might be some sniffy people out there. But, you know, the fact is that I've won about 10 awards for what I do in science communication and that kind of thing, including a medal from the Royal Society. And most people would say, well, actually, it was worth a gamble because the group I set up helped to be one of the first people ever to be doing podcasting. We created the first ever journal podcast. We went up to a journal and said, 'let's make a podcast with your content each month or each week'. It was the first journal to do that. We broke through so many boundaries and borders and created new things and started doing things in new ways that actually, nowadays, people come to me and say, 'how will you come and work with us to promote what we're trying to do in our department?' I think people now realise the value of all of this.

So, it hasn't been a challenge for me, because we were out there first. And it's always easy to win a race when there's one person racing and that's you. If you don't win, there's something very wrong. Right? If I was coming along now, I don't think we would get there. I don't think it would happen in the same way. We wouldn't have the success we did because the competition has become absolutely enormous. And so, it would be very hard to vindicate ourselves in the same sort of way. But I think people do appreciate the value of this and they do appreciate the fact that there has to be some people who are ambassadorial. And if you ask a university, 'how much do you spend on trying to recruit people to your university or your institution', or 'how much do you spend on press and publications and PR?' And, actually, you'd be very surprised by the amount of money that goes on that. And then you say, 'how much does this [podcast] person cost? Who does this?' Well, not very much in comparison. And so, I think the value is obvious.

Chris Smith, The Naked Scientist

00:35:50,000 I'm not just doing a podcast, I'm also doing things that highlight my platform and uplift my profile in ways that positively reflect on my institution and my department, that can be used as a spotlight that ultimately go back to things that reflect tenure. And I think that when junior faculty have that in mind and when senior faculty can actually see the merit in what they're doing from that perspective, they go from like, 'oh, that's crazy,' to like, 'wait. That's actually really smart.' Because it actually is super smart for someone in a precarious situation to make everyone think you're valuable.

Liz Wayne, PhDivas Podcast

00:19:14,000 I suppose at some moment, without our knowledge, we started to be recognised as the *contrasens* group. People were recommending us. A friend or a professor was taking us to a party or meeting, and saying, 'hey, here is Marina from *contrasens*, they are doing this great thing'. When you are so young and you feel like you didn't do anything significant, it's already a way to be seen.

Marina Mironica, contrasens

00:03:08,000 It always has been a hobby. It's not something that I know is going to make lots of money, but I think it's a really good opportunity, at least from a selfish standpoint, to meet really interesting people. It saves on money, you know, not having to find a rich uncle to pay for conferences that I can't go to that I'm not even interested in.

Ann Wand, Coffee and Cocktails

00:01:52,000 It was back in 2015. I finished my PhD, and I got a postdoc in Japan at the University of Tokyo. And, so, my wife and I moved to the University of Tokyo, or to Tokyo itself, and we didn't know anybody. It was the first time I ever stepped foot in Japan. And the only person I knew was the person who agreed to host me at the University of Tokyo. You know, I'm American, you can probably tell by my accent. I was educated in Hong Kong, my wife is Australian, so I was living in Australia. I had this broad network, but nothing in Japan. And so, I was a bit concerned about moving to a country and maintaining this network that I had established over the last 10+ years and my wife basically said to me, 'why don't you start a podcast? Because that's gives you an excuse to talk to people in your field and maintain those ties'. And I thought, 'oh, that's a good idea'. I mean I love listening to podcasts.

Will Brehm, FreshEd

00:19:19,000 Especially as an early-stage researcher, it gives you a reason to go and talk to people, especially at these mega conferences. So I've printed out some stickers with the logo, and it's a very easy opener or an icebreaker to go in and talk to someone who you don't know and say, 'hey, do you listen to podcasts? I do this one, would you like to be on it?' and then it gives you a concrete reason to follow up. And even more than that, it gives that researcher an output for their time. And I think that's a key aspect. You know, having coffee or, you know, 'can I ask you a few questions via email?' The person you're asking usually doesn't have much time, gets no concrete deliverable for their time, whereas with a podcast, they have something they can send to their department in their performance review, they can use it in their teaching for students. So, I think that's a really key point.

But going back into how it's benefitted, I think, to kind of pivot off your question a bit, I think it's more about the practitioner outreach. So academically, it's given me material that I've used in papers with people who are outside of academia, so industry practitioners, but also people who are working in different government institutions or who are working for campaigns or advocacy groups. That kind of niche audience is part of the podcast audience. I've been invited to events outside of academia. So more like communication conferences for practitioners where then you become the scientific expert, which is kind of fun. Which is also something you wouldn't have access to necessarily just by publishing papers, so I think at least for me, that's important because it's related very much to the topic of the podcast, which is how actual practitioners are campaigning. This has given me a foot into that which both informs what I do for a research side, but also establishes a network outside of academia, which I think is really crucial, at least for what I'm doing.

Michael Bossetta, Social Media and Politics

00:01:49,000 I was a professor [laughs]. And as I became professor, one of the things I noticed was that we were required to write these long and sometimes interesting books. And nobody ever read them. And nobody is, of course, an exaggeration. But very few people got any value out of these books. The primary value of these books was to get people jobs and tenure. And as credentialing devices, I guess that's fine. But I was thinking that this was an awful waste of what might you call it, social capital or something like that, because a lot of money had been invested in me by the U.S. government to train me as a Russian historian. And I didn't really feel like the people of the United States were getting their money's worth. So I was thinking to myself all along, 'how can we get the information that is trapped in these books?' and I used the word trapped advisedly, and I'll come back to that, 'out to people that might be interested in it?' And you might well say, 'well, nobody could ever possibly be interested in this', and I would say, 'well, I thought that, too. But I conducted a big experiment over about 10 years and I learnt I was wrong'.

00:08:33,000... [in about 2007] I produced my first podcast, which is called *New Books in History*. It was as an experiment, I just wanted to see if somebody would listen. I didn't know if anybody would listen. And this is basically me talking to other academic historians about their new books. Well, people did listen. You know, I stuck them up online and I put them on *iTunes* and people listened. And that was pretty gratifying. And over the course, the next three or four years, I conducted a couple hundred interviews, and I made every mistake you can possibly make, which is how you learn how to do something. So then at about 2010 or '11, I had a 'if not me, who? If not now, when?' moment. And I'd just gotten tenure, by the way. And I said, 'you know, I really should do this.' So, I resigned my job and I devoted myself after that full time to podcasting and building something I called the *New Books Network*, and the *New Books Network* really, for those who don't know, and that's everybody, it's really just a lot of podcasts, like *New Books in History*. They are hosted by academics usually or sometimes graduate students, sometimes writers, sometimes practitioners. There are about 250 volunteer hosts. They sign up. I train them. They usually do them, I don't know, in their offices or in their bedrooms. They record all the audio. They set up the interviews. They get the books from very generous publishers. And then they send the audio files to me at *New Books Network* central.

And I do all the audio editing, which is most of what I do with my time when I'm not working one of my three day jobs. And I manage the websites and so on and so forth to make sure that their word gets out. We produce five interviews a day now. Every weekday we publish five interviews... our listeners download over a million episodes a month, and it's growing pretty rapidly, organically. We don't buy advertising. I think we're achieving our mission because a lot of people listen and the ideas that would have been trapped in these books that people don't know about, and even if they do know about them they couldn't afford them because they tend to be quite expensive, well we set these ideas free by talking to the people that invented them. And it's very gratifying work. I get a lot of fan mail. I don't get any money, really, but I get a lot of fan mail. So that's nice. So, Ian, I'm sorry to go on for so long there, but that's the story.

Marshall Poe, New Books Network

Generous

Opening Scholarship

I love the fact that I can find scholarship everywhere. I love the fact that when I find it, if it's done half decently, I can listen to it and not only understand it but also get lost in the ideas it generates with and through my own thinking. I love the fact that when I'm on a night bus to Bengaluru and unable to sleep, harangued by sounds vibrating from the nose of the gentleman to my left, and by my body's transformation into an ungainly concertina of pain and regret, I can drift on and on whilst listening to experts deep dive into birds, brains, or British imperialism.

There's a lot of slightly disingenuous buzz around 'open-access' scholarship because it's available for free. I'm not sure how 'open' I'd call the scholarship if it's drenched in impenetrable jargon or if the journals or publishers took thousands of pounds in author processing charges (thus limiting who can publish there). Radically insurgent open-access projects like SciHub make a large chunk of pay-walled content free in any case.

Podcasts can make scholarship open not only because they are free to listen to but also because they liberate knowledge by showing the world how truly wonderful and beautiful the topics we work on are; by bringing diverse voices and perspectives into dialogue with academics and putting ideas into public spheres that might otherwise not be heard; by allowing the people we work amongst (or experiment on) to understand and enjoy our work; and to open up our scholarship to scrutiny and discussion by the public whose taxes pay for a lot of our work (whilst recognising that being able to find time to listen to long-form podcasts is a privilege exercised by those with certain types of jobs or lifestyles). And this is why podcasting can be central to a scholar's work.

Here's the amazing thing about scholarly podcasts when they're done well: they can be long, detailed, extremely complex, and yet understandable. I can listen to five or more hours on religious legal activism whilst cleaning the flat, defrosting the fridge, and descaling the kettle, but I'll leave a podcast after minutes if I get lost in a jargon quagmire. There's too much good stuff out there in the world to waste it on listening to scholars who haven't bothered to think about their audience.

Fairly well-educated people should be able to understand scholarly work – maybe not the details of methodologies or minutiae of theoretical contributions, but at least the big picture and nuance of the arguments. Podcasts can open this up to them. And podcasts can also be the platform for those with great ideas who struggle with written English to speak to wider audiences. Because, even though there's great science journalism out there, there's also limitations on what it can do with and through conventional media, especially when it comes to presenting multiple angles on a topic, or embedding new research within its wider context and debates. This can't be left to shouty podcast hosts who draw in listeners by telling them what they want to hear. Rather scholars can, and I would say should, be the bridge between difficult-to-comprehend research produced in text form and publics who hunger for deep, complex, yet accessible knowledge.

Why is it important to put scholarship into people's ears?

> 00:15:55,000 Maths has this PR problem. Your whole life as a mathematician is going to cocktail parties and telling people what you do. And they say, 'oh, I hated maths'. You know? And then you get used to it after a while. But, you know, maths is really beautiful.
> **Kevin Knudson, My Favorite Theorem**

> 00:50:52. OK, let's be utopian. I think it can liberate academia. It can provide a space to do the things that academia says it wants to do. It's actively a way to reach outside the walls of academia in terms of where your content goes and where your knowledge goes. It's

an active way to cultivate and welcome diverse voices, either through decolonising the curriculum or actively employing people from different backgrounds and celebrating and supporting their work and their voice and their perspective. I think it's limitless potentially.

Neil Fox, The Cinematologists and podcast scholar

00:30:07,000 I'm the only, kind of, academic podcast in China. But podcasting is on the rise in China, but most of them are chatting about not very important things because, you know, the censoring is quite intensive in China. You cannot basically talk about anything serious.

Zhang Zahn, Tianshu

00:33:23,000 For me the excitement lies not in its ability to disseminate things differently, although the accessibility of that format means that it is, but actually, in terms of what it can do to enliven that process of knowledge production, both for within a community of scholars, but also perhaps to the people that we're working with [researching amongst]. You know, I can't remember the last time somebody I'd done research with actually read something I wrote for academic publication... I think that podcasts also offer that opportunity, particularly when you're thinking about participatory forms of research, where people could listen to what you're thinking about and can come back and go, 'well, actually, no, I don't think that's right. I actually think it's this.' It could form a way of engaging more people in the participatory dimensions of an ethnographic project in some respects.

I actually think it's crucially important to think about what it does to scholarly practice and what it does for knowledge production, because otherwise all this discussion about alternative modes of dissemination, I think, quite often present alternative modes of dissemination as somehow apart from a project. But actually, a project starts when you think of the idea in the beginning, and it goes all the way through for as long as you're prepared to talk about what it is that you're doing.

Michaela Benson, Brexit Brits Abroad

00:23:03,000 The podcast just makes so much sense to me, because I'm not only writing about it, I'm also trying to impact the world [laughs] – the universalist world that cannot see anything else than economic growth, progress, or technological innovation as the only path towards sustainable living. So that's my political project in this. I don't know if it's answering your question, but it's kind of a world-making-practice podding, making these voices available to others, strengthening these alternative voices.

Maria Ehrnström-Fuentes, Världar i Omställning
[Worlds in Transition]

00:49:14,000 The voice really relates to the political dimension of academic knowledge production in itself, which is irradicably linked or inherent to this practice, or to academic knowledge in itself. It shows the illusion that academic knowledge is pure and objective. It is not a very popular way to say it, especially not in academia, but particularly with the movement *March for Science*, with the idea that we have to now go to the streets to say, 'believe us, we are the scientists'. But at the same time, no one gives them the reason to believe them, to believe their knowledge. Because how could they understand it? In natural sciences, there are some very abstract concepts, some theories, some modelling. No one understands! Not even those people who are doing this themselves always understand it. And how could we? If we're not more transparent, more open, and particularly if we're not reflecting on the political dimension of this process openly, even being open to criticism. So, I think it is immensely important for academia and academic knowledge today that this political dimension is made public, open, free, and accessible to everyone, not only younger academics.

Moritz Klenk, Podlog

00:03:33,000 I don't know how this is going on in Hungary, but in Brazil, there is this very strong and anti-scientific atmosphere at the moment. The president [Bolsonaro], he does a lot to help that. So, science, people doubt it, people think it's too expensive, people think it takes too long to present results, all that kind of thing that I think you're familiar with. And that really strikes us. And I think it's very important that we stand up and defend the university and defend science and defend anthropology.

Of course, I do understand when my friends and colleagues in science and technology studies, and anthropology of science, for example, they say, 'I don't want to be together with all kinds of science, you know, I don't want to be with colonial science, I don't want to be with science that just goes over people and doesn't respect them, you know?' Of course not. But as a principal, as a value, I think universities and science are very important.

We receive public money and I think that we have the responsibility of being accountable for that. And that means we have to learn and put into practice the communication of our results. Anthropology is a science that needs sometimes 300, 400 pages to write up results. I mean, the monographs are our cherished kind of writing. Of course. But who reads 400 pages? We have to be able to write smaller pieces, communicate in a better way. We have to put our carnival on the street.

Soraya Fleischer, Mundaréu

00:31:25,000 Listening to a podcast is something that people do when they're doing something else. So, it allows you to get into people's minds at a time that neither video nor writing would allow. So, it's usually done when people are driving or exercising, and it comes with that sort of baggage in terms of it's usually a privilege to have that much time to do other things and listen to podcasts. But having said that, I think it still allows you to access people's times, people's minds at a time when they're relatively unguarded.

Sarayu Natarajan, Ganatantra

00:31:44,000 So we produce knowledge in so many different ways, it's hard to pin them down, and I'm someone who thinks we shouldn't pin them down. There is no one perfect or no universal knowledge production process. We all produce knowledge in different ways, and most of them are valid. And we also disseminate knowledge in a whole bunch of ways: we teach people in our classes about it, we write research papers, we go to conferences, we talk in the media, and we also now make podcasts. And I don't think that any one of those is more or less valid than the other. They're all just different modalities for communication. So, therefore, I think podcasting is absolutely core business, like absolutely core to what we do.

Dallas Rogers, City Road Podcast

00:23:50,000 I have a very strong belief that a scientific study that cannot be understood by a lawyer or a doctor or any other highly-educated person is probably not very valuable. It's less valuable because there's some wall of pretence that's cutting people off from the meaningful insights that you're trying to develop.

Joseph Cohen, The Annex Sociology Podcast

00:48:59,000 I do understand why journals exist. Why the review process exists. A lot of people put a lot of unpaid, very dedicated work into all of those review mechanisms. But at the same time, I also think it is worthwhile having complementary modes of sharing knowledge that don't require the same kind of input and resources, but that nevertheless hopefully get some level of engagement going. I don't know about you, but I regularly have taught classes on academic writing to incoming master's students who sit in front of me circa week two or three of the academic year and go, 'What are you making us read? These academic papers are just unintelligible for the most part. I've done a degree, I've worked in different industries, but it takes me forever to try and work out what this person is trying to say'.

Judith Krauss, The Convivial Conservation Podcast

00:45:01,000 It's so much more accessible, actually, for many of our Indonesian guests to come and agree to speak with us in an interview than if we said, 'can you please write that 500-word piece?'

Jemma Purdey, Talking Indonesia

00:17:26,000 But one issue I have is that a lot of the articles of scientific journalism will just take one study, they take one study and they're going to talk about the results of this one study. But they fail to be able to talk about all the other research that has been published in this area in the years past or the context of this one study in the entire area. And only an expert scientist can really understand the full picture of that. And a lot of the time the scientific journalists are very good in that they can interpret the scientific findings, but they're not an expert in the area. And so sometimes scientific journalism can be misleading because all they're doing is they're cherry-picking one study and saying, look at the findings of this one study. They're not necessarily giving us the whole big picture. And why? Because giving the whole big picture takes a lot of effort. And I don't blame them because who is willing to put in that much time and effort to understand a complete area and give a whole big picture? It takes a lot of time, and scientific journalists don't necessarily have that time. So, with the podcast, that's what I try to do. And I think that is the big missing gap between scientific journalism and what experts can do in a podcast.

00:23:41,000 And in regard to having the general public choosing, it's difficult. And that's honestly one thing that we struggle with, because the reality of the situation is we are competing against people that will give science through rose-coloured glasses and tell people what they want to hear. And, unfortunately, those people are the ones that gain a strong following, that are heard the most, that have the loudest voice, because people always want to have reinforced what they are already believing. And as scientific communicators, if we are going to make it scientifically rigorous, we're not always going to be telling people what they want to hear. You know, I'm going to share the potential negative side effects of an intervention. I'm going to tell you the clinical trials that had the negative results where the treatment didn't work out, and people don't always want to hear that.

Stephanie Caligiuri, The People's Scientist

00:02:11,000 There was a public sphere where a lot of discussion was taking place, but it wasn't being influenced by the academic sphere, which had this depth. In the sense they could both very well feed into each other because we felt a lot of academics did have something to say. They would have a lot of nuance and depth to a conversation, it's just that neither of the two spheres knew how to get to each other.

Alok Prasanna Kumar, Ganatantra

00:25:22,000 It was my way of saying, 'well, I know that I am not going to be an academic, but is there a way to think about sharing all of what happens in an academic setting with an outside world, with somebody in the outside world?' I don't know if that makes sense, but it was my way of saying, 'let me be that bridge', because I can engage with academia and I can also engage with the outside world through the work that I do... It was very much that sense that I can, and want to, be a bridge. I know I'm leaving something behind, but I really don't have to leave it behind entirely.

Sarayu Natarajan, Ganatantra

Cultivating Listenership

I remember being excited the first time someone read something I wrote and tweeted about it. I'd written a chapter about vigilantism in a smaller Indian city for an edited volume, and a student had read it, taken a photo of the last paragraph of the introduction, and tagged me saying something complimentary. In trying to think about why I was excited (banishing the idea that I might be a little bit of a loser from my mind), I realised it was because I'd just had an interaction with a real live human about something another human (me!) had published that wasn't mediated by the often-dehumanising conventions of academia.

And podcasting, because of its seriality, because it is deeply entwined with other digital media, and because of its intimacy and vulnerability invites responses from listeners that articles or chapters do not. This allows scholars who podcast to get to know and interact with their audiences, to nurture relationships over time, to draw sustenance from the togetherness of some online interactions, and to better understand why and how people are drawing on their work.

If you work full time in academia and say you have time to keep up to date on the latest research in your fields of interest then you're lying. I never lie. I read for very specific purposes – for whatever piece of research I am planning or writing up – but I miss finding out about the sort of great scholarship that pushed me to give up my career as a professional footballer for Liverpool FC and become an anthropologist.

Listening to podcasts is an important way for scholars to find out what their peers are doing outside the annual big conferences. Producing podcasts is an impactful way to speak to the small group of humans on our planet that shares a similar set of intellectual interests as we do.

How do podcasters interact with their listenership?

> 00:05:59,000 We got to know our audience over the years because they started writing in and telling us about themselves, we've done a few surveys and it really goes from high school kids, college kids in all fields, graduate students, professionals, academics in all fields, not just science, we have health care workers, we have IT people, we have labourers, we have trash collectors, and house painters, and so forth. That's amazing, frankly. And now we're getting hundreds of emails a day. And I'm learning what an amazing gamut of people are listening. I think we could probably be better, but it's not bad in terms of educating people.
>
> **Vincent Racaniello, This Week in Virology**

> 00:11:40,000 There are days, especially early days when there weren't very many academics podcasting their lectures, when I would get ten or fifteen thousand downloads. It would just happen and I'd go like 'Why? Why?' But people wanted to know things and I would get emails from people, everyone from a cable installer in Denmark who told me he was installing cable TV while listening to me give lectures, which I thought was fine, a long-haul trucker from Australia who I'm still Facebook friends with. I get emails about once every couple of months now from somebody saying, just 'thank you for doing this'. A lot of them, I would say half the emails I get are from students at other universities who say, 'thank you for doing this because my prof is really shitty'.
>
> **Dave Brodbeck, Spit and Twitches & creates**
> **podcasts from lectures**

00:49:23,000 A difference that I find in podcasting as opposed to other forms of media, is that it's ongoing and it's audience building. It changes the expectation of what any single episode needs to accomplish. If you can bring an audience along with you and educate them slowly and make them feel like they're part of an in-group with you and growing along with you, then you don't have to explain every single word that you use every time.

Ian Pollock, The Familiar Strange

00:15:13,000 There was a wonderful element. It was almost like a club feel to it in the early days. Once upon a time, we ran a message board just for our podcast that we maintained on our website... and at one point I felt like I knew every single person on that board when we had 2000 listeners and maybe 40 people on the board ever. I didn't know any of them by their real-world name, but I felt like they were all friends by whatever Internet handle they were using on our message board. It's funny to have evolved with it at that slow of a pace and have those memories. It really does seem like the way somebody would portray it in a movie someday on the early days of podcasting.

Dan Carlin, Hardcore History

00:34:30,000 We've actually surveyed our listenership and what we know basically is that a third are students, a third are teachers, and not just university teachers, but also secondary and primary school teachers, and then a third are what I guess you could call development practitioners. So, people who work for the World Bank, people who work for the U.N., people who work for NGOs [non-governmental organisations]. And each group sort of uses the podcast in different ways, of course. For me, what's interesting is the development practitioners simply don't have time or access to academic literature. They don't have the time to read it. They don't have access to it. But they know how important it is to inform their practice. And so, the podcast is a really great way for them to learn about new ideas in education and help them identify which papers they should actually spend more time reading.

Will Brehm, FreshEd

00:28:01,000 Initially scientists wrote each other letters to try and communicate what they'd done to each other. And to me, this is just a different way of doing that, it is just a different format to do that. And rather than the scientists themselves writing, they're telling us the story and then we're trying to tell it to everyone else.

Nick Howe, The Nature Podcast

00:53:26,000 I think that the great value in podcasting is what is called 'narrowcasting'. And that is creating content that is relevant to a small group of people, but it's highly relevant to them… and it provides those people with a sense of community. And it provides them with a kind of constant flow of content and discussion about something that they find highly relevant. Similarly, with South Asian studies or Southeast Asian studies or Russian history or whatever happens to be. Small groups, but the people in those groups really want this information. The problem is trying to find a way to pay for it because the groups are small. And so, they're not going to attract sort of run of the mill advertisers. The big advertisers are going to go for the big podcasts.

Marshall Poe, New Books Network

00:00:19,000 I could list 100 reasons why downloads are not important, but I'll only name a few here. First, the main beneficiary of your podcast is you. So if you are learning from it, networking with it, and, most importantly, having fun, that's really most important.

I know it sounds cheesy but it's 100% true. And there's not much you can really do about download numbers. I've tried everything – mainstream media pick-up, plugging on other podcasts, promoting at every talk I give and nothing moves the numbers significantly in any direction.

It's really about the quality, not quantity, of your audience. If your podcast is reaching 50 people, but they are peers or students in your field, your content is going directly into their ears, and they're going to be appreciative. One email about how much someone appreciates your podcast is worth thousands of downloads, and even with a small audience, I get those emails quite regularly. And I think, it's also important to visualise your downloads as people in a room. After 5 years, my core audience is maybe 500 people. But imagine speaking to an audience of 500 people in person. Most of us will never have that opportunity in an academic setting. But with podcasting I do it regularly.

So I check the downloads every now and then just to make sure that nothing's wrong with the podcast technically, but I've really come to view downloads as otherwise not important.

Michael Bossetta, Social Media and Politics

00:02:39,000 I started to develop a cognisance that I was having impact in the field, in a weird way, in a way that I hadn't anticipated. And it started to become a professionally rewarding activity. And we sort of just kept on doing it. And we accumulated followers…

…You know, more people listen to any individual podcast I produce than any of my written work has accumulated in a lifetime. The platform has become surprisingly large. Our podcast is small by conventional standards, maybe we get about a thousand listeners an episode, but compared to other sociology specific academic outlets, we're very, very large. That's like three or four main stage plenary sessions at the annual meeting. It's just become a meaningful activity that we've decided to continue.

At the beginning it was a disciplinary service, which, as you know, in the rank of things that professors have to do, it's something that your employer values the least. And it is just not something that traditionally we've been pushed to prioritise in our productive work. It felt like a hobby. But as I experienced more of the podcast, I came to see it as very meaningful, as an opportunity to play a very meaningful role in the discipline. And I found myself situated at the centre of a lot of exchanges. If you have a podcast and you have listeners who are on faculty at every top university in your profession, then the discussions that you have and the messages that you transmit will be sent to every department.

And sometimes you debate issues, or you arrive at conclusions, or you have arguments about the discipline stuff that might not fit in a journal, might not be picked up in other directions and it's just a very fast way of processing information and sending it out. And if people hear it and act on it then you've pushed the discipline in a small way…

00:06:05,000 … What is sociology? At its root, there is, what, three, four thousand sociology professors in the United States? American sociology is what we collectively say it is. It's collectively what we agree it is and what we tell our students it is and what we write it is. And so, the discipline exists in our collective minds at any point in time. We tend to think of scholarly activity is cumulative. And it's like Marx wrote this, that, you know, somebody else wrote this, she wrote this, etc etc. But it doesn't really work like that. We ignore huge parts of our tradition. We just shed them. You know, before it was the American Sociological Association, I believe it was the American Eugenics Society. But eugenics fell out of favour, and so we've wiped that from our collective comprehension of what our discipline is and what we're about. It still exists, in fact, in our history, but it is not an active or meaningful part of our discipline because the people who are practising it now do not treat it as such. We don't communicate it as part of our history. You know, we don't push people to integrate it in whatever we're purveying as the sociological worldview.

And so, my opinion on podcasting and blogging and a lot of these new media, these Web 2.0 outlets, is that they push the collective conscious of the, you know, two, three, four thousand people who are entrusted with the discipline and who get to say what it is. Then you are moving the discipline. You are affecting what sociology is said to be and what sociological information is being conveyed through the universities, you know? And so, if you're pushing the discipline then it is impact, right? I mean, it is impact, you're pushing it. You're moving opinions of the practitioners. And I mean, that's what a journal article is in effect. That's what a plenary session is. It's an attempt to convince your peers that something's true or that, you know, that we should be thinking a certain way or doing something. And so, if you separate it from the medium and just look at the action that's being performed, it strikes me as meaningful.

Joseph Cohen, The Annex Sociology Podcast

00:34:51,000 Just having that mouthpiece, having the ability to influence and shape conversation and to comment on what institutions are doing, whether that's universities or whether it's subject associations, whether it's journals or whatever. We're very much now a player in the field and we get cited in existing scholarship and we make it into lectures. We're sort of like an unofficial commentary darting about from place to place, popping up. Guerrilla scholarship is maybe a good way to describe it [laughs].

Chris Cotter, The Religious Studies Podcast

Creating Communities

Communities can be terribly exclusive and hierarchical formations, they can also be caring, nurturing, and horizontal (and a mix of both these and more). The community at any one scholar's department or university, within a field or discipline of study, or in a classroom or reading group can make certain constellations feel more or less welcome and engender more or less generous forms of intellectual engagement. The creation of communities through podcasting does not necessarily have to be a normatively 'good thing', but for many it has been a way of creating communities that sit askew or half-in half-out of academia's existing community structures. Maybe because of this, or maybe because it creates new networks of knowledge exchange, podcasting provides them with the intellectual and emotional support that they could not find elsewhere.

Linking ideas across and between scholars and schools of thought can be engendered through podcasting, but it needs conscious effort if it is not to reproduce existing hierarchies. Podcasting practices that intentionally search for communities outside the mainstream can be a way to discover who one's allies are in academia and also be a way to build and nurture relationships that go beyond the workplace, as well as creating space to hear from younger sets of scholars aside from the 'usual suspects' (as scary as this can be for some).

In what ways is scholarly podcasting creating communities?

> 00:22:44,000 I like to think that podcasting can't entirely be consumed by academic audio culture. I hope it can't become like an audio book version of an article. That interests me less than this idea that we're creating community, we're creating empathy and we're trying to find a more richly human way to interact with each other than just as professionals or specialists.
> **Dominic Boyer, Cultures of Energy**

00:11:37,000 We're trying to build a network between these academics. Let's say we have Christian B. Miller on his book, *The Character Gap*, doing some brilliant research in virtue ethics. Well, we've got this other scholar, Rutger Bregman – the Dutch historian – who has this brilliant new book, *Humankind*, and again, whether humans are good or not. We'll compare Bregman with Miller across the episodes. We'll say, 'You're saying something completely different to what Christian Miller told us and listeners a few months ago!' And, so, it's that cross episode discussion – which not only creates that network between them and clashes ideas in a way that they're never going to have a chance to in academic publishing, but at the same time, it creates a really brilliant sense of community, like listeners are getting the latest research.

Jack Symes, The Panpsycast

00:19:34,000 There's more to say as well because the way in which the podcast is created is also problematic because it is very Western-centric. It's in English. It's two experts talking to each other. It gets disseminated around the world. So, it doesn't actually incorporate more of these Southern theories and these Southern voices. And often that's an issue of language, that's an issue of technology. It's not as though I don't want to bring people from all over the world on, but oftentimes it's just not even possible. We are fighting against only having a one-way path of knowledge, it's production by these, you know, Western academic experts, and then it gets passed on around the world and that is problematic. And so, we're exploring ways to sort of create at least a two-directional path. Or maybe even a multi-directional path in terms of knowledge production. And that's where we are currently in our thinking in the podcast.

Will Brehm, FreshEd

00:08:35,000 I want to engage with queer communities, minority communities, other marginalised groups within academia. I'm a biracial person. I am a queer individual. And as I was approaching my last few semesters of undergrad, I was starting to make a decision if I wanted to pursue grad school and stay in academia or if I wanted to get out and go make money. And across the board, I felt a lot of trepidation about what my experience as a queer brown person would be in either of those spheres. And I found it very difficult to just find people that would be able to interact with me in that honest way that I needed them to interact with me. And so I was trying to brainstorm, how do I get these people to have some honest dialogue about what it means to be a minority group, working in academia, working in different STEM [science, technology, engineering and mathematics] fields, and sort of break down that initial barrier of like, you know, well, we have to talk to H.R. first, 'here's our diversity and inclusion statement'. You know, I wanted to get past that. Like we all have that. We all know what that is. So I created *STEMS and Leaves* with the intention of exploring intersectional stories and STEM. I left it a lot more broad to give myself room to work with, but even that, using the word intersectionality, pretty clearly focuses on what I'm about.

Ezra Mattaridi, STEMS and Leaves

00:17:55,000 I was really depressed in academia. I was having problems with all of the academic knowledge production processes, and that is the reason why I love podcasts so much, because… it helped me get over a really hard time in my life and reconnected me to academia just because the people I interview are from academia.

Since the whole production procedure, at least for me, I don't know how others do it, but for me it is a long procedure, and it involves my interviewees at every point.

They send me their work that they want to talk about. I read their work. I write questions. I send them questions and we discuss the questions together. We add some stuff, subtract some stuff, then we have the interview, of course before that we talk about how the whole procedure will work. Then we have the interview. Then I edit it. I edit the whole thing, but don't add the introduction first. Just the main body. I send them the main body, then we have another discussion about what to keep, or if they want to add something, they think maybe they didn't explain a point enough, so maybe we re-record like 2 minutes, 3 minutes together again. Then I finish the main body. Then I record the intro, then send them the intro. Then we discuss the intro again. Then I combine all of the things. Then we discuss the title. So, the whole procedure for me is very 'intimate', it helps me to spend time with them, discuss with them, which really makes me energetic and really happy because we don't discuss it in a way to please anyone. That is my point. We don't try to please any literatures. We don't try to please any advisers. We just do it.

Mert Koçak, Sexuality and Gender in Turkey Podcast

00:53:37,000 I mean, I think that the main thing that I have taken away from this experience so far is the opportunity to be generous and helpful to other scholars. There's two ways of being a scholar. Or there's at least two ways of being a scholar. But we know one way is you can be the person who spends all your time talking about yourself and your work and why you're great and why your work is great and why people should pay attention to you and so on and so forth. And that works. That model works for a lot of people.

But there's another way. You can also talk about why other people are great and why they're interesting and why their work is great and why people should read it. And I think that that model works, too. And

I think it works in a lot of ways, a lot better. And I think it enables you to think about who you're talking about and why you're talking about them and why you're making the choices that you're making in terms of who you're talking about.

And one of the things that we really tried to do in podcasting, in thinking about who we want to listen to and why we want to listen to them is to say, 'you know, there's a lot of people talking loud all the time. Who aren't we hearing? Whose voices aren't getting heard? Who isn't getting an opportunity to speak? Who isn't getting the platform they deserve? What kinds of ideas are we not paying attention to? And how can we highlight those voices as opposed to the ones we hear from plenty?'

It's one of the reasons that at the end of the day, I am glad that the work I'm doing is not institutionally sponsored, because if the University of Kentucky College of Law were sponsoring this work, they wouldn't let me invite a transgender Asian undergraduate to be one of co-hosts. They wouldn't let me give the opportunity to an incarcerated person to do a series of podcasts about the ideology of the Latin Kings. They wouldn't let me post random LPs from the '60s of weird documentary recordings of police officers. They wouldn't. All the things that it's so easy for an institution to say 'no', but it's so easy for a person to say 'yes'.

Brian L. Frye, Ipse Dixit

00:31:22,000 I would say that one of the things that podcasting and anthropology does is create a new set of people that students and scholars have heard of. You know, there's always been a sort of a tight sense of who the superstars in anthropology are that everybody cites and everybody reads their work. And to have your name be known opens up the possibility. It doesn't end there, you then have to go on and do good work, but to become somebody that another person would say, 'I know about your work. I'm interested to read the next thing that you write', that's something that not everybody has had access to historically. The people who are cited the most, for the most part, come from a very small circle of universities. And they all cite one another. And so, I think an important way to look at podcasting is as an addition to academic publishing. That allows for new voices to be heard and to circulate in new ways.

Ian Pollock, The Familiar Strange

00:36:35,000 We can all think that some of the most prominent voices in your discipline are not the people who are full professors. There are a lot of junior people, more precarious people, and I think that podcasting, the rise of academic Twitter, is allowing for the prominence of voices that is not based on seniority anymore. And I think that it doesn't upend the hierarchy, if anything it just allows the precarious to have more of a voice, but I think it speaks to, perhaps, the continued structural precariat of academia, that people want to have their voices heard. Because getting an academic job, even getting on the tenure track as the beginning of a permanent job, is so out of people's reach that they are also just trying to do the work that makes most sense for them and that nourishes them.

Christine Yao, PhDivas Podcast

00:41:32,000 I think that the other thing with the students and postdocs and stuff, I think that often – and I don't know if that's in every field, but particularly in astronomy – once you reach a certain level in your career, you do a lot more supervising, you do a lot more lecturing, and a lot more administration, management, that sort of stuff. So, in our career or in our field, a lot of the real cutting-edge work is happening with people between 25 and 35. So it's PhD students and postdocs, early career researchers. And they don't often get the press. In order to try and get across the really interesting stories, it's good to look at these young people because they're the ones actually doing the work. They're the ones who sit at the telescope. They take that data. They reduce it painfully over months sometimes, they know every little part of it and then they find the interesting stuff, which then they analyse and, with a little bit of help from their supervisor, put into a paper. So when there's a big discovery, you don't want to go to the leader of the project. You want to go to the guy who actually dealt with it. Who sort of knows the ins and outs of it.

Daniel Cunnama, The Cosmic Savannah

00:45:31,000 Yeah, exactly, I mean, academia is so hierarchical and, you know, not to disrespect people in the high positions, because many people have worked very, very hard to get there and many people are doing an excellent job there and mentoring the younger career researchers, but it is also very easy to abuse your power at the highest level, even without realising it. And so, we don't discriminate. Of course, we interview professors and high-level people. But as [co-host] Dan [Cunnama] said, when there is a story, we generally try not to go straight to the top. We try and find someone who's worked intimately on it, but maybe not in the public eye already.

Jacinta Delhaize, The Cosmic Savannah

00:15:34,000 I find younger and more junior scholars do more show prep, they put more effort into making the show a success. I've interviewed people who were quite notable in the field, and I found them so disinteresting that I never published the episodes. It was very self-referential. And, you know, they turned it into a biography. And it's just sometimes people who are famous do not fit well in all formats and they definitely don't fit well in ours. We try to level the playing field and make things informal and conversational. And I think people who are used to being fawned over can adapt to that, but they don't always adapt to it well.

Joseph Cohen, The Annex Sociology Podcast

00:17:16,000 What kind of emerged for me as a theme was that I realised almost all the people we'd interviewed, that they were terrified. They went through like all the series of emotions. They were excited to be offered the opportunity. They were terrified of the platform. And part of that is about the type of scrutiny that women receive as a public intellectual. I think about online hazing, the Twitter storms, and then also added to that just what academics are kind of told about how they present themselves.

I think people in general struggle with having to communicate their knowledge and sometimes academia tells us not to do that. And so, doing a podcast, which is not inherently like a peer-reviewed journal article is like, 'oh, wow, I am allowed to do that?' 'Am I actually an expert?' Talking to people about that process for them, what their fears were, but then also having them come to the realisation that the podcast is actually good for them.

Liz Wayne, PhDivas Podcast

00:29:49,000 We've asked a lot of different people to be on this podcast, and I've asked a lot of PhD students and also postdocs, but they're the ones who are the most sceptical and least willing to come on the podcast, because it's like, 'oh, I don't have anything interesting to say'. Or you can tell that they're very worried about being judged or that they're going to compromise their position on the job market if someone hears their podcast.

Stefan Partelow, In Common

00:56:34,000 You know, I strongly feel that what I am doing is disruptive and that it is shaking up a long-standing tradition where undergrads shut the fuck up and listen. And it's shifting power to the curious who will ask their questions and they will pursue answers.

Ezra Mattaridi, STEMS and Leaves

3   What? A Curiosity Generator

The creative, transformative, and generous practice of scholarly podcasting helps create the conditions for scholars to follow their curiosity. Scholarly podcasts are thus curiosity feeders and, because they open new possible avenues of interest as they go, they are also curiosity generators that provoke changes in ways of asking, forms of knowledge production, and modes of knowledge creation.

> 00:32:42,000 My parents have this old award that I got as a kid in like the third or fourth grade from my teacher. It said 'most inquisitive', which I think was the way of saying 'most annoying'. And I think it's just something I've always done. And it's just like, how do I scratch my curiosity?
> **Matt Candeias, In Defense of Plants**

> 00:21:33,000 It's providing the fora for academic research to be heard outside of the journal, outside of the book that very few people pick up, outside of the special report that was written for an NGO. So, it's not new, but it is really quite hidden knowledge. If together we are illuminating and profiling that research, then that feels pretty good. As [co-host] Dave [McRae] was saying too, that's just driven by curiosity in each of us in our own ways. As hosts of the podcast, we are curious and want to know answers to questions and

DOI: 10.4324/9781003006596-3

that's why we select the guest that we do. As Dave said, we get the freedom to choose our own guests. There's no one producing it and giving us tasks. We want to have a certain percentage of Indonesians, a certain gender diversity, apart from that, there's no limit. We are driven by our own curiosity and interests and that's what it's all about.

Jemma Purdey, Talking Indonesia

A Way of Asking

Dynamic Conversations

Of all humankind's creations, pubs are our greatest – greater than the wheel, fire, and RSS feeds. Not bars with loud music and people in loud shirts, those are terrible. But cosy watering holes with cosy corners, where you can get deep into a conversation and be nourished for an entire evening on deep cups of curiosity.

And some forms of good scholarly podcasts can feel like listening to parts of such a conversation, only with someone who has spent a lot of time researching something and with a potential audience hanging in the background. And when it's brilliant, which it often is, you can feel a podcast host's eagerness overtake; they excitedly ask questions that they've had in their head since they read a scholar's work, either to satisfy themselves or, if they also know a lot about the subject, then for an intelligent friend who doesn't. And good questions can create new thoughts, which lead to new questions.

And if you imagine yourself listening in on these conversations, then also think just how amazing it is to listen, not only to people speak about things they have spoken about many times before but also to hear them think out loud as their conversations go on and on. If they go on long enough, and are taken to places they didn't imagine, and are spurred on by dialogic immediacy, then sometimes knowledge is produced.

What's so great about conversations?

00:01:53,000 We [co-host Anindya Raychaudhuri and I] were eventually based in Edinburgh at the same time and we were both working in St. Andrews. So, we started carpooling. And one of the things that I think characterised our friendship from early on was a kind of a sceptical but still active interest in critical theory. And we both came at critical theory from different perspectives but had a shared sort of appreciation for what it can do for us and for our work. Because we share similar politics, that was part of it as well. It takes about 90 minutes to get to St. Andrews from Edinburgh, depending on traffic. So we'd have these long extended car conversations and sometimes a conversation would continue over the course of a week or, you know, a few days in the car and we'd bring in perspectives from other people... and then I left St. Andrews and started working in Aberdeen. And it was this kind of massive hole, I think, in our friendship that all of a sudden, we didn't have the thing that brought us together every week. So, no matter how busy we were, we had a car chat at least once a week for a few years. And because I'm a kind of narcissist at heart, I was like, 'We could set aside time to have our conversations, but record them and then our friends can listen and then tell us what they think'.
Hannah Fitzpatrick, State of the Theory Podcast

00:02:38,000 Well, why do I podcast? I think because I learn quite a lot and, actually, it is a kind of joyful exercise. That doesn't mean that it is not also quite a lot of work, but that it is an opportunity to learn about people and their work and their ideas and their theories that I might not encounter otherwise. There is an impulse to go out and find new work, and find new scholars, activists and artists who I might not otherwise be searching for. I think of it as kind of an auto-directed masterclass in a way. We have the opportunity to go out and find new work, new books, new people, new ideas that are evolving or that are being put out into the academic world or the para-academic world and read those things more deeply, come to get to know those people in more intimate ways through the conversation, to ask questions that we might not be able to ask otherwise.

We all have the experience of working in pedagogy and teaching and reading a text very carefully, sharing that text with students, having a wonderful conversation with students around any particular text, and there's some aspect of that in the podcast.

But the next dimension is that in the podcast, you actually get to speak to the authors themselves. You actually get to talk to the artists themselves and say 'what were you thinking when you created that composition? What were you thinking when you used this example or why did you pick this particular historical period?' And we don't typically get to do that when we're simply engaging with texts in the classroom. It's like a supercharged form of learning in a way because you have the opportunity to engage with these people very directly.

Cymene Howe, Cultures of Energy

00:14:05,000 I think part of that is asking the right questions and putting yourself in the mindset of the audience and being like, 'if I was listening to this for the first time and I had absolutely no idea what this was about, what would be my questions?'

Nick Howe, The Nature Podcast

00:24:50,000 It's been really essential that we have the duo thing going on, because [co-host] Philip [Shane] does ask me the questions and points me in directions that I would not have thought to go otherwise but turn out to be really essential. I've learnt a lot about the kinds of questions that people are interested in thinking about and also the kinds of answers that they're interested in hearing too, and that I find engaging.

Matt Stanley, What the If?

00:04:45,000 Philosophy as a discipline: podcasting is perfect for us. It's the best way to convey philosophy. Philosophy is a conversation you have with yourself, or other people, and it's supposed to be dynamic. When you're reading that paper in a journal, you want to say, 'Can you explain a little bit further?' You want to say, 'Have you thought about this?' Those questions you ask yourself and leave on the PDF, they jump off the page for the listener! It's how it should be, and how we want it to be.

Jack Symes, The Panpsycast

00:31:34,000 If you do the questioning correctly, it should lead you to thoughts. And because they're questions, I'm not giving you answers, but thoughts that maybe you hadn't considered that whole avenue... I overuse the example of that moment in the film *Planet of the Apes*, where you see the Statue of Liberty sticking out of the sand and you go, 'oh, my God, I never considered that my civilization might fall'. And then all these dominoes start tumbling in your head and you see things differently. Well, those are things you can insert into the conversation as a non-expert in a non-expert way.

Dan Carlin, Hardcore History

00:23:22,000 It's listening to people think, which feels really like a privilege; asking a question and hearing someone really engage with it in real time and feel them working out an answer and then being pushed on it. That feels unique. I can't get that across in a written interview. It's different to watching someone on film do it. The intimacy, particularly the headphones experience of listening to people think, is very private and very, very privileged and that feels kind of special. And when [co-host] Dario [Llinares] and I are making our podcast, we're always trying to include that sense of you're listening to people formulate ideas, or crystallise ideas, but not trying to edit out everything that kind of conveys that.

Neil Fox, The Cinematologists and podcast scholar

00:12:30,000 It's not just dissemination, in part because the format of the interviews has been essentially a conversation. It's not extracting information, but there is co-thinking going on during the conversation. I view this as a bit of an ideal, we have some ideas when we go in, but ideally you help guests think through new ideas that maybe they didn't have before, or ways of understanding their own work that they didn't have before. That's part of the ideal, is that it's not just like, 'OK, now tell me these things that you could have just written down'. It's rather, 'let's get some more together in a conversation'. And so, I think that's where there is new knowledge produced. And you don't get there immediately.

It's also been humbling to me realising that to get to that space where knowledge is being produced is not automatic. There's a path you have to take in a conversation to get to that space. [Co-host] Stefan Partelow had this really cool idea to make these 'Insight Episodes'. And I view that as distilling the parts where there really is a lot of knowledge being created. You know, this 10-minute segment that took half an hour to get to. I can tell when it's happening, 'oh, OK, now this is cool. Now we're kind of co-realising something'.

Michael Cox, In Common

It does take a way to get there. They're never in the first 15 to 20 minutes, you've got to get warmed up. You've got to prime the brain and get a prime speaking and the engagement before you usually get there.

Stefan Partelow, In Common

00:22:50,000 I think that there is a performative nature of giving a paper at a conference because you are separate from the audience. There you are, the paper giver, and there is a discussant who will give you some comments and it's kind of a static situation. And I've also been in some workshops that are better because it's a more structured conversation that compels everybody to read the paper and come in with comments on each other, and so that's a more dynamic form. The traditional panel is a little stuffy, generally speaking, and even if you are a more relaxed paper giver, you're still giving a paper. Whereas the podcast, and again this is how I kind of try to think about it, the podcast is an opportunity to have a conversation about something with somebody who is an expert. I often find that my podcast, after I finish recording them, I'm like, 'OK, we've bounced in 14 different directions in the course of that 45-minute conversation that didn't necessarily take us through the book in the table of content order of it, but we had a really great discussion of what the research was about and why it's important and why it's interesting and how the author got to it'. And to some degree, I guess it's also the way I think. It's more interesting to me, and I'm hoping, to listeners.

Lilly Goren, New Books in Political Science

00:29:50,000 So writing: you would read a piece, cite it, critique, agree, disagree, simplify, whatever else, but you would do it only in the textual form. So, there is not that speed or there's nothing emotional about that whole process of writing when you write about somebody's text. That critique process is slow, it's dry, it's not engaged, it's not fast. So, both of these did not necessarily seem like great ways for us to engage with academia, whereas audio allowed you to do a bit of both. It allowed you to have the ability to reach out to a wider audience and then it also allowed you to have a faster sort of conversation or chat about somebody's work. It allows you to be informal. It allowed this engagement. You could bring some levity into conversations about fairly serious topics, which is sometimes necessary because they seem so insurmountable and so difficult to conquer.

Sarayu Natarajan, Ganatantra

00:09:13,000 I've thought about this a lot, especially when you go to a conference, and they have one talk that's like 'the public lecture'. And the conference bills it: 'this is us reaching out to the local community'. And you go to the lecture and the scientist, if it's a bad one, sounds bored or like they're hedging everything because they're nervous about their audience, they're nervous that there's someone else who's an expert that's going to do that, 'this isn't a question, it's more of a comment' type thing. And so those can end up being really stilted. And I think then people think that's what academia is. And it's like, 'no, no, no, you've got to come to the bars after the conference. Some people are like ripping on some idea they think is stupid or getting overly excited about this really cool new technique. Like, that's when you really see what science is, it's this creative excitement of talking to other people. They're just expert enough that you're all thinking about this in different ways and getting new cool ways that you could implement it in your work'. That's honestly part of why I wanted to drink on my podcast. I want that, that kind of 'in the bar after a conference feeling' when you're really getting to the nitty gritty and thinking about cool new things.

Sadie Witkowski, PhDrinking

Engaging Storytelling

Walking into school with my son at 7:15 a.m., my mind still groggy from sleep and not yet soggy enough from coffee, he begins to tell a story. As the words cascade onto each other through his facemask like lemmings fighting past each other to a cliff's edge, I realise he's told me the ending of story already and now I'm getting a blow-by-blow account of what happened in a game in a courtyard between children whose names he's neglected to tell me. If he were a podcast I'd turn him off, but luckily he's not, and so I enjoy the account of a game I can't get the name of.

After I drop him at the gates, warning him to stay away from drugs and girls, I walk into work, getting blown along the bank of the Danube, listening to a scholarly podcast, and thinking about engaged storytelling. On some level, I tell myself, all scientific communication, but especially a medium like podcasting, can be considered a type of storytelling – they can inform and entertain at once with an awareness of the logics of stories as they unfold through narrative and interview formats.

How do scholarly podcasts and storytelling entwine?

00:43:32,000 Every version of doing science to me is telling stories. Whether it's podcasting or writing papers and doing experiments. In my opinion, the best scientists are very creative people who could probably write pretty solid novels if they would have gone down a different track. I know when I'm writing scientific papers, I'm very conscious to be trying to tell a story. I mean, it can't be mostly entertaining because that's not the point. But if it doesn't have a dimension of keeping the reader engaged, it won't have its effect. And so the podcast, it's not scripted, it goes its own way, it's organic, but I still think that we conceive it that way. We work a tonne, we work really hard on the front end to make sure that – whereas we allow for flexibility in the guest to talk about things that they get excited about – we make sure we're gonna hit things that will leave listeners with some cohesive message.

Marty Martin, Big Biology

00:29:24,000 So I think of myself as a storyteller. But the goal of the storytelling is to envelop people in both the art and the science of teaching and learning. So I don't want to pretend that the science isn't there, but I also don't want to bore you to tears such that you would never want to learn more.

Bonni Stachowiak, Teaching in Higher Ed

00:20:14,000 When we're teaching audio storytelling, we're teaching them how to find that moment of pause and what interests them.

We do a lot of interviews on a food truck, so we'll have interviewees make us dishes on the food truck and we'll record them. It becomes like a cooking show/history show. We do a pre- and post-interview about their lives, but in the middle, they're cooking something. It becomes this kind of narrative tool that we can utilise while the meal is being made, we can jump around throughout their life or add historical context.

We don't just do interviews. I do a field recording course as well, because having some action, having someone make food or do something or do a tour of their house or the restaurant or what have you lends itself to segmentation, which is also something that draws people in. So, there's an art form to trying to create these stories. And I feel like the audio lends it-self to telling those stories when we can actually get up and go and do things and be in the now, and then also go back in time…

But finding the right time period is difficult. We can only talk about this time period from here to here, and we might be leaving out some context along the way. And that's hard, I find, when it comes to, you know, putting a podcast together, because there's stuff I want to drop for the sake of the narrative. But then again, this is why we utilise footnotes within our scripts or little notes or sources or other add-ons later in the books or stuff like that we can follow up on. We can't put everything into a podcast, but this is why I'm trying to find and why I'm teaching the students to find that one thing, that moment of pause, that one thing you want to explore and then expand on it. You don't want to have a series of things that you're pursuing or it becomes too convoluted, too much stuff, you know, and we're not looking to do like a three, four or five parter of certain topics. We want to touch on them and then maybe we'll add more within other media like a book or a story map or something like that.

Kent Davies, Preserves and podcast instructor

00:33:48,000 I think it's definitely great to have a podcast be a spark for a conversation and a jumping off point, but in terms of creating a narrative podcast or making any kind of documentary it's not a choose your own adventure, that's not satisfying for a listener. You have to pick a viewpoint. You have to make decisions and pick a story and pick what story you're telling.

I think a lot of people are surprised, and I think I was even surprised when I was in journalism school and I learnt this, that even true stories have all of the same elements as any other story. Someone else might talk about their research and it might be interesting, but it doesn't have the ingredients that we would need to cook it into a podcast. And that doesn't mean that it's worthless, it's just not going to make a good podcast.

You are taking the listener or the viewer along on a journey that you have created. Someone has carefully crafted a narrative and now you get to listen to it and enjoy this thing that we made for you that's going to take you on a journey. But it's so much easier to do than films. It's so much cheaper. You don't have to go to all these different places. You don't have to have this incredibly expensive equipment. For us, as a history podcast, we get to tell stories that happened in the past and make them feel like they're present. The example that comes most clearly to mind is in one of our episodes about opioid addiction treatment. There was a character who was talking about his early days in this commune treatment centre in the 1960s in San Francisco. And he just so beautifully described what it felt like to be in this rundown warehouse building and the mouldy food that was going bad and how there's only one bathroom. He just painted this picture. It was even better than looking at pictures because it was helping create a picture in the listener's mind. I think it's just so powerful to hear people's personal stories. There's nothing like hearing it from someone's own mouth.

Mariel Carr, Distillations

00:22:43,000 The sound is the very first thing. I'm working at the moment on a podcast with people who come from a film and television background, and it's bewildering to me because they've written an entire 20,000-word script outline without having done a single interview, really. Because they're used to working from shot lists because everything is so expensive you have to plot out the story in advance and then you go and fulfil the story. Now, I don't like that approach at all. I like to work organically. You go out and find the people to interview and then they lead you to somewhere else. And around them you find the sound. And then out of that, you sit back and analyse what you've got and then devise a thematic or episodic structure or whatever it might be.

But, you know, good sound. So sounds like cicadas are great, just that tinny sound. If I ever hear them on a summer's evening I will just stop what I'm doing and record them. Sometimes the wind really howls in that funny way through a house, you can actually hear it like a cry, and I'll capture that. Although that's a tricky one. Things like sirens. Sometimes you will get five or six fire engines racing past because of some incident, I always get that because that can be a metaphorical sound. I mean, I do believe in authentic actuality, but sometimes you can actually play with that and have an authentic generic sort of sound. There's the sound for the sake of sound. That is beautiful sound. And then there's sound that you get as meta scenes or actuality that paints in a bridging picture around whatever your focus is, be it a person or a theme.

Siobhan McHugh, documentary podcaster
maker and podcast scholar

Active Listening

It's great that you can listen to podcasts everywhere. However, this may give rise to the suggestion that podcast listening is not 'serious scholarly listening' that 'serious scholarly work' deserves. It's true that, for the most part, people are not sitting in libraries or at their desks taking notes on what they listen to (but some people do this apparently!).

Listening can be engaged, however, in a different way than through note-taking in libraries. It can be an active, yet relaxing form of listening as it is free from distractions that digital reading is resplendent with, with listeners seemingly happy to have deep, complex explorations into topics for many hours at a time. But listening to podcasts can also activate the mind as listeners have visual images painted for them by podcasters or fill in the gaps that are left by the open-endedness of some audio creations.

How do people listen to scholarly podcasts?

00:29:54,000 I skim read when I read articles, whatever, news. So, I read it quickly. I try to get out the interesting point as fast as I can, and then I'm done and then I move on. But with a podcast, and I know people listen to podcasts on double speed, but I don't, I listen to them at true speed – and you just have to lean in, relax and let the information flow. And you can follow the story, you get taken on a journey and you don't know where the journey is going to go. But you get this whole experience out of it. Whereas reading an article, I get three paragraphs in, and I kind of understand what they're doing, where they're going, and then I stop. With a podcast, I don't do that. I listen through to the end because it's a journey and I want that experience. It's kind of a shared experience with the people you're listening to.

I find it incredibly relaxing because it does slow the pace, even if I am doing something else, it slows the pace of my mind. My mind isn't hopping around so fast trying to get the next thing, the next titbit of information. I have to just slow down and follow this one story, it's like reading a novel or something, like reading a book. It's slow. It's calm. It's relaxing. Podcasts, I find, are relaxing even if they're intense.

Daniel Cunnama, The Cosmic Savannah

00:29:27,000 Yeah, I think podcasts, in general, they just fit very well into the current times because people, they want to make the most of every single minute of their day and get information all the time, so when you're on a treadmill or when you're running in a park or cooking or doing a puzzle or whatever, you can listen to podcasts and get information all the time. I think that makes it very attractive because you can't read a blog article when you're running in a park or whatever. But at the same time, and quite contrary to that argument that I just had, it's also a medium that slows you down. You can also enjoy podcasts very relaxingly, right? Sitting on the couch and listening to two people talk, it's very calming in a way. So, it has two opposite effects, I think, on its listeners. It's either very efficient or it's the opposite, and I think that makes it very attractive and it just fits very well into our time.

Johanna Sebauer, BredowCast

00:00:05,000 So we had an *Introduction to Development Studies* class that was offered well, for decades. And it was only done in person. What we did a couple of years ago was actually look at offering an online version of it. And there was some negative feedback from that. One of the things that people found was that the use of the online software was too intense. So, you had all sorts of things coming up at the same time, you had to tune in at a certain time to catch the lecture. The instructor was doing it from a camera like this, only angled to see his nose hair and part of the ceiling. And, you know, it was basically a repetition of the book, the textbook. And amid that, there were also other distracting elements as well. There wasn't a lot of enthusiasm for this course.

So when we started to get this feedback I went to my friends who are broadcasters, I do a lot of work on TV and radio as well, and they said, 'well, think about this. Think about where people are learning online'. And we're seeing it right now in the pandemic. People are huddled up on their couches. They're angled terribly on their beds. There is not the proper ergonomics going on with it. And there you've got all these issues. But outside of it, people are ultimately in isolated environments when they're learning online. And that is where the wheels come off the bus because if an instructor thinks that they can get up and communicate to someone in an isolated environment with a busy screen in the way that they can command an audience of 200 people in a lecture, they're done. And I think that's where a lot of the frustration with online learning gets in and the reluctance, both of instructors and students. So, talking to broadcasters, they said to me, 'well, you know, the one medium where people consume the best in isolation is radio. We've done that for 100 years, and storytelling for the thousand years before that. Why not find a way to make the podcast or the radio the core essence of an academic course?'

And that's not a new idea. I mean, they did that in the Soviet Union and Cuba and Vietnam, and they would have university courses over the radio. People are working away, they're doing their thing and what it does is that instead of looking at a screen or a course environment that's so busy and then getting distracted, the podcast is the distraction. You can drive, you can do dishes, you can get your meal ready, you can walk home and you can listen to these podcasts at your own pace. They're asynchronous, you do it as many or as few times as you feel comfortable and go from there.

Robert Huish, Global Development Primer

00:17:24,000 We used to go to extremes to try to appeal to 'Joe and Jane public' such that the first ten episodes we used to produce a long and a short form of the episodes. The long form is basically the same thing we do now. It's mostly an unedited release: have a conversation, put some music in and that's about it. But the short form was really demanding on us. It was very distilled. We made a very, very strong effort to make it approachable by anyone, such that we would spend in some cases an extreme number of hours trying to perfect a script, to communicate really complicated types of things that we would discuss with our guests. And we stopped doing that, not because we didn't want to get the audience, but it blew us away when we looked at download statistics and the long-form ones were something like twice as popular as these short-form ones.

Marty Martin, Big Biology

00:26:02,000 The main thing I think I've learnt from podcast audiences vs. just the general people reading articles is that a *Conversation* article on average is going to get way more clicks, so arguably reads, than a podcast. And that's inevitably because it's very easy to just click on an article and skim it over and get a sense of it, whereas a podcast is a real investment and what everyone says is that podcast audiences are a lot more engaged. You know, it's much more of an intimate thing where someone is talking in your ear. But, for us, the reason that we like to do them is that they enable you to properly explore topics in depth in a way that you can't with an 800-word article.

Annabel Bligh, The Anthill (The Conversation)

00:28:38,000 I think listening forces you to interact a lot more. Well, if you're not looking at your phone while you're listening to a podcast, if you're just listening to it, you kind of have to throw that mental picture, you have to help with the story, you've got to throw that mental picture in your head of what's going on. You have to argue through what's happening if you're confused. Sometimes I like the purpose of confusion or 'where are we going with this?' because it really kind of excites me, it has that moment where it draws you in. So, yeah, I think, listening forces you to engage, provide that mental picture, connect to the story in your own way.

Kent Davies, Preserves and podcast instructor

00:22:44,000 People who use audio, they have to know to be visual, it's sort of counterintuitive. And I'm also a super visual, almost predominantly just a visual thinker. But I'm not talking about having to make gestures so much as I need to see pictures. For me, I have to have a scenario as a story, something happening so I can imagine. If we're going to talk about how big the space station is, I need to create a situation where I'm on it and I need to walk across it.

Philip Shane, What the If?

00:16:23,000 Once you remove this hard visuality that we all have to embrace in the world that we live in, what does that open up, and what are the gaps that are left there? We could do this layering of sound that had an indeterminacy to it. This idea of emergence; a space left in where people are going to subconsciously engage with the different layers of audio in different ways and create their own pictures and bring their own selves to it, which you do with all media, but there was that indeterminacy there with sound that was a bit more open-ended.

Oliver Rick, Somatic Podcast

A Form of Publishing

Without Gatekeepers

Editors are wonderful people. I also wear an editor's hat sometimes. And, when they do their job well, they serve a really important purpose, making sure the good stuff reaches our ears and eyes.

But, of course, they often don't. I've been asked to review a piece which, after reading, I said I didn't think should be published, but the guest editor went ahead and published it anyway with only minimal corrections. The guest editor has since published with and gone on to work with the person. I'm sure they sleep well at night in the comfortable bed the decent job bought. Which is my slightly snarky way of saying that there are also a lot of people who misuse their editor's role, and others who block brilliant research from being published (never mind the peer reviewers who think it's their job to find why something shouldn't be published, rather than trying to understand what the researcher was trying to do and pointing out how to achieve it). But as

I said above, journal articles have a purpose; however, they cannot be the be-all and end-all of scholarly publishing.

And this is one of the reasons why podcasting appeals to a lot of scholars. They can speak directly to their audience with no gatekeeper, and whilst such a publishing mode might seem normal to younger generations, it was impossible until a short while ago. And sometimes a research field moves so fast that scholars want to get the research out immediately; they want to go deeper into a topic than a publication might let them and produce niche content for such small audiences that commissioning editors at mainstream presses would turn away. But all this means that there are fundamental challenges to questions of authority, who wields it, and how it's asserted.

What's it like for a scholar to be able to publish what they want and when they want?

00:46:03,000 I think it's also fair to say we're working in a landscape where the public are asking questions about academic research. How to produce academic research for the public in responsible and ethical ways is something that I really think we need to take control of. And that is a conversation that we need to be part of because there are plenty of people who are using that alleged academic expertise to quite different ends, shall we say, without wanting to get too judgemental about them.

There are interesting questions about the role of intellectual work in public life and how you do that. And there are obviously different scales at which that happens. There's a real tension: you want to communicate complex understandings because this is, actually, a public landscape that doesn't encourage complex understandings. If you can't come up with your two-minute speel, then you're off mainstream media. First of all, you're out of *The Guardian*, which is probably the only side of mainstream media that you might even want to consider being part of. And there's someone else occupying that space and communicating that knowledge. And the great thing about podcasting is, it's not really mainstream; there is still a space for more complex understandings. I've written for *The Conversation*, I've written for *Open Democracy*. And there are questions about who's in control of knowledge production in the same way as you'd have with mainstream broadcast journalism. You know, who is doing the editing? I've written for the BBC, that was a fascinating process. But, you know, there is a danger that those complex understandings get written out under the guise of making things accessible. And so, in a way, being able to control the medium, being able to control the content of the podcast, is quite useful in some respects.

Michaela Benson, Brexit Brits Abroad

00:01:33,000 It was, and I remember this really well, 1998 when I first started doing this kind of thing. And it was for what was *National Science Week*... And this call went round the university: 'will anyone do some talks?'... I was real interested in the nervous system and how the nervous system worked. And so, I said, 'I volunteer, I'll do a talk'. And I dreamed up this system so we could actually make a system to record how fast information travels through the nervous system. And long story short, having almost blown up a lecture theatre in the aim of trying to make people jump and then ask, 'I sent you an auditory stimulus. Your muscles responded. How long did they take to do that?' I kind of realised that this was quite fun, making science interesting, accessible and really opening a door and a window onto a sector of the world that most of the general public would never have the chance to step into.

And so, when the university came back to me a year later and they said, 'cor, that was really good last year, we'd do the same'. I said, 'yes, but I don't like doing the same thing again and just repeating myself, let's do something different'. It was the GM food scandal and there were loads of pictures in newspapers and journals and things, lots of misinformation about DNA technology and its uses and its abuses and so on. And I thought, well, actually, most people had never seen DNA and it can't be that difficult to dream up a protocol to make something or do something that would enable people to see it, but also to take the experiment away and do it at home.

So, I spent the weekend in the lab just fiddling around with ingredients to get a really efficient protocol. So, you could take pretty much any foodstuff, use my protocol and you'd get handfuls of DNA from whatever that foodstuff was. And I did this as an experiment, almost like a cooking programme on telly where you see them chatting away as they chop up bits and pieces... And in the audience was this radio producer who said, 'will you come on our radio station and talk about what you've been doing? Because it's seen as pretty interesting and unusual. Never seen anything like this before'. And I went along to a small commercial radio station and appeared on this guy's programme for what should have been five minutes... turned into about two hours of science questions, answering things that people phoned in with, a bit of music, and just some general chit chat about science. And they said, 'well, this is really interesting, we should do this again'. And so I said, 'yeah, okay', because I hadn't really appreciated quite how powerful a medium radio is. And so I went back a week later and I dragged in a couple of other PhD students from the university and it went really well. And so, we started making programmes initially on radio because at that time there wasn't very much science on the radio. There was certainly not on commercial radio and certainly none on local commercial radio stations.

And after doing it for about six months, we thought, 'well, why are we appearing on someone else's programme competing with Britney Spears, 7 Club Seven and Geri Halliwell for airtime. Why don't we actually petition for our own programme?' And so I managed to convince the management of the radio station to sell me a year's airtime. And I went around and raised all the money. And I bought a year's airtime off them to create a dedicated science show on a Sunday evening.

And off the back of that, then thought, well, why actually just stop with radio? Because the Internet's got sufficiently powerful now, this is around the year 2000, that we can actually offer people things for download and they... [can] download something in less than a century because, you know, we were beyond 42k dial up by that stage. And why don't we just offer them the programmes and let them take them away and do whatever they want with them. And so, we started just making these science radio shows on a Sunday evening and then we'd put the whole programme on the Internet in a format people could download it, take it away and do whatever they wanted with it. And it just took off.

And as soon as the whole notion of podcasting got invented, we're already there because we'd already actually come up with a way of enabling people to subscribe to this stuff and get it delivered automatically to their computers. So, after that, it was relatively easy to just translate what we were already doing and to make it compatible with podcasting.

Chris Smith, The Naked Scientist

00:08:36,000 I think [co-host] Stefan [Partelow] is right, knowledge is a public good, that's a common framing, the question is: how do we produce it? I think an additional challenge we have is that academia is essentially an arms race. Frankly, I think we have a culture of overproduction. I think this is exacerbated by things like ResearchGate and Google Scholar. I think those are unhealthy. I have accounts in them, of course, so we're all a little hypocritical. I look at Google Scholar pages now and I see 25 publications in 2019 and I'll see ten already in 2020. I think that's stupid. And I think that's an appropriate word for it. I'm fed up with this idea. We tell our students not to worry about grades and then worry about our own similarly myopic criteria for success. And everyone's writing and no one's reading because everyone's writing and no one's reading. It becomes self-reinforcing. And for me, it's getting off that treadmill myself a bit, but also, as Stefan said, since no one's reading, maybe they're listening.

In a lot of the episodes, I'll talk to this person, and it's very humbling because I feel like when we get in our own tracks, we get caught up with our own thoughts and maybe some of those thoughts we find really interesting and that's cool. But there's some really incredible people out there, and I hear them talk on these episodes and it's amazing. It's really wonderful to hear just someone else's really interesting, well-thought-out ideas, and that's something that we don't avail ourselves of enough as we're trying to just crank out the next PDF, because that's what's made legible to other people because they're busy cranking out their PDFs.

Michael Cox, In Common

00:32:13,000 In theory, you can take an interview and publish it within a couple hours, which is an extreme case, but especially in this field of social media, which is moving so quickly, the platforms are changing every day, to get something in the present and distribute it within a week to put the forefront of knowledge, you know, to put knowledge that is currently preliminary results or in the revise and resubmit area or what have you, to get that out there is precipitating publishing time by months. And I think that's important.

It also gives a forward-looking approach to what academics are thinking about, so where the field is moving. If you read something that's just been published, just released or you see something at a conference, you're still not getting the thoughts about where that research is moving. And so, you can dig that out in a podcast, even if the ideas haven't been tested yet. You can see what those researchers are thinking about in light of their previous results. What would they adjust? What are they testing now?

Michael Bossetta, Social Media and Politics

00:47:57,000 So instead of just reproducing what the media reproduces in terms of these publications and press releases, we give a different story which can undercut the media perception of a big discovery, too. You can show people that there is more depth to it than just this high-level stuff. I've found those sorts of articles, the ones you see going around when there's a big astronomy discovery, incredibly frustrating because they don't have the right information. They have the information that the media thinks that the public wants to see. It's such a structured thing like, you know: introduction, here's a quote from the leader of the group. It's boring and it's actually not what the public wants.

Daniel Cunnama, The Cosmic Savannah

00:19:17,000 I do know that a big part of our audience is people in their 40s and 50s like us. And it partly could be that many of our references are to things of our own generation, but I also think you get to a point where things aren't made for you anymore. Like when you're young, those very basic shows on television, all of which are great, they work for you. But as you get older, you've seen that show so many times and you want to get a little bit more niche and you might subscribe to magazines, like I subscribe to *Scientific*

American and for me that would be my limit, but I can follow it. Podcasting has filled this incredible niche of 'a little bit more, a little bit deeper' than your average mass market show.

Philip Shane, What the If?

00:09:39,000 Part of it is, I think, people under-estimated how interested the general public are in science and technology, medicine. And when podcasting came along, suddenly there was this objective measure of how much people were consuming things. And if you look at the numbers for downloads, for science programmes, they're really high. And people suddenly thought, 'well, people are downloading this. They're not just downloading a programme because it is a good programme and it's got a bit of science in it. And just it just happened that because the science was in a popular programme, the science ends up popular. There are people downloading science programmes. Isn't that amazing?!' And I think that gave people confidence. And so podcasting has been great in that respect because it offers a more objective way of measuring audience responses. I think that's partly it. I think also the fact that the technological revolution around us is selecting for people. It's basically nurturing an interest in science and technology because people are seeing the difference it is making to their world. You know, there are more smartphones on Earth now than there are people. Not everyone's got one, but we've made more than there are people. And we think about 80 percent of the population of the UK have a smartphone. Now, that's a very big penetration of a technology into society. So in other words, you've got technology that has the ability to deliver this sort of information to people at people's fingertips and in their pockets.

Chris Smith, The Naked Scientist

00:36:56,000 The relationship to authority or rigour and its connection to the way in which the information is uttered is something I think that needs to be continually challenged. Not that authority in-and-of-itself or rigour or expertise, god forbid, is something that should be thrown out of the window. But I think that correlating that with certain ways of presenting, certain ways of speaking, often leads you to associate that with certain identities and certain systems of thought and certain institutions. And I think that's the problem, when those correlations are made, are rigidly accepted, and if anyone tries to challenge that, it doesn't have the authority that it should.

I think it is a sort of broader problem of the digital age, isn't it? Little thought experiment, let's say you get rid of all legacy media and you say everything now is online and everything that you read lives and dies by its own context. So for example, you wouldn't have an article that is written by *The New York Times* automatically having an authority attached to it because it's with *The New York Times*, you know. We've moved into an era now where even those connections in terms of authority are being challenged. It's really problematic because it moves you into the arena of nothing is trustworthy anymore.

I think it's a really difficult question, but I am interested in challenging the idea of, 'OK, I'm an academic, I have to speak in certain kinds of ways in order that my "authority" will be acknowledged or taken seriously'.

Dario Llinares, The Cinematologists and
podcast scholar

Asking for Evaluation

The problem – you might be screaming at the book, with having no so-called 'gatekeepers', you might be screaming a bit louder – is that we need some way of knowing what is decent, legitimate, well-thought-out scholarship and what is a podcast made by a person who is clever enough to make a decent argument but not humble enough to admit he might be wrong about a study as he screams into his mispositioned Blue Yeti mic about how 5G spreads the coronavirus.

Yes, I don't scream back at you, I agree, but the old ways of evaluating scientific output don't fit the medium of podcasting. We need some way of evaluating and reviewing, but we scholars should be in charge of developing what those might be (not people who don't understand our disciplines), whilst also recognising that because podcasts promise freedom there's plenty of people who don't wish to submit their podcasts for evaluation or review and that's totally and utterly fine. But for those of us who do, we need to think about how (and when) podcasts might be reviewed.

How should scholarly podcasts be evaluated?

> 00:37:55,000 If there is a body of academic podcasts, there'll need to be some way of ranking or evaluating to say, 'hey, was this helpful or is this just a dude with a microphone who had a bit of a chip on his shoulder?'
>
> I think that when we see the measurements come into any sort of system, it's because you get a certain amount of charlatanism that gets in there. I'm thinking back to how medical schools at the turn of the 20th century were highly unregulated. You know, you could just pin your sign up on front of your door and say, 'it's Ian's Medical School' and there it is. And it wasn't until the Carnegie Foundation did a massive report in 1910 that looked at the quality of medical education that standards and review process started to come in. So right now, I think you've got podcasting as sort of a side dish to the main meritocracy of academia – how many articles, how many books, how many conference presentations, how many grants? That's still how we're evaluating each other. So you do a podcast that's popular. 'Yeah. Cool. How's your tenure file going?

Nowhere? Awesome'. But if these things start to become more of a core practice and it does influence teaching and it does influence research, then my guess is there is going to be some form of evaluation that will follow it. That tends to be how the university rolls.

Robert Huish, Global Development Primer

00:16:32,000 And I think that's a really useful thing to think about as we are starting to explore possibilities for peer reviewing podcasts is that we really need to ask ourselves not what is 'the cookie cutter one size fits all' approach to peer review, which is an incredibly, incredibly recent invention.

Hannah McGregor, Secret Feminist Agenda and podcast scholar

00:19:11,000 And that begs the question, will there eventually be a sort of standard or checklist to evaluate a podcast as an academic output? You know, the legitimacy of it, the rigour of it etc. As podcasters, as practitioners, I think that's what we fear. But I also think that we need to be open to considering that. If that's what we have to do to make this 'legitimate', then let's have a look at how that could be done. And maybe as podcasters/scholars, we can have control over how that's done as opposed to handing over that control to, you know, the bean counters.

Lori Beckstead, podcast scholar

00:40:25,000 I don't view this as an academic output. This is by no means meant to be of the same standards of research or, you know, going out for peer review. I think one of the great things is that it's not being externally assessed. A couple hiccups in the editing or, you know, a fan blowing too loud in the guest's audio, you let it go and the audience is quite forgiving. I don't view this in any way to be a research grade output. To an extent it's also a form of entertainment as well. You know, it's a very nerdy form of entertainment.

I don't even think about that. I try to make interesting material that brings out, you know, interesting parts that relate to current events or relate to research. But I mean, I totally said some incorrect things on the podcast. And I don't go back and re-record them later or go back and dig back into my files and make sure that I issue a correction statement, because I don't think that's solely what the medium is about.

Michael Bossetta, Social Media and Politics

00:37:20,000 I think academic podcasts, like papers, need to be criticised. Like now H-Net has a podcast section. The Oral History Association has special issues and sections and publications with reviews and criticism. And that's got a lot better.

It's OK to criticise the podcast. I feel like the first step in granting legitimacy to these forms of digital scholarship is having forums where people can criticise them like you would any kind of peer-reviewed publication.

I think we put ourselves in this position to get peer reviewed by just having transcripts and footnotes. And they should be making arguments on certain things.

I think taking the time to do transcripts or any kind of contextual documents, having a list of sources available and just pulling back the curtain, showing how it was created and why it's being created, what are the research questions they're pursuing. Having all that in one place will make it easier for people to review it, I think.

Kent Davies, Preserves and podcast instructor

00:09:02,000 The big idea: the *Open Peer Review Podcast* is what it's called… the idea is that a researcher would be invited onto this podcast to talk about a particular project. And there is a host who is aware of what the research is about, but isn't necessarily an expert in that particular field. And then the researcher invites a peer reviewer. Much like, you know, at my school, when you are applying for tenure or promotion, you get to nominate several people who are experts in your field to review and evaluate your performance. In that same spirit, the researcher asks a peer reviewer to join them on the podcast. So there's the host, the peer reviewer and the researcher.

Beyond the standard academic journal or a publication, I believe that podcasts just in and of themselves can be considered a legitimate academic output. However, what I decided to explore with this particular project is how could podcasting assist on the way to publication. What role could podcasting play pre-publication? Assuming that a scholar still would like to publish in the traditional forms, what could they do with podcasting before that? The idea is to have a conversation pre-publication where the peer reviewer can ask some questions. You can have this conversation, this dialectic, and it affords an opportunity for the scholar to think about their work in different ways, to be able to leave from that conversation and perhaps go back and polish what they're doing or rework some things, reformat things. And the idea is that it's an opportunity to have that conversation and then be able to have an even better shot at publication in terms of having already had some peer feedback, and being able to have done some review and some polishing and some editing based on that.

Lori Beckstead, podcast scholar

00:07:14,000 And that summer before I started my job, I struck up a conversation at a conference with the Senior Editor at *Wilfrid Laurier University Press*, which is a university press here in Canada, Siobhan McMenemy, who is really interested as an editor in what it looks like to create more broadly accessible scholarship. They're doing all sorts of really interesting work. They've created an audio book line. They publish a lot of scholarly books that they work really hard to push into trade discovery systems. So, you'll like find them at a regular bookstore, you know, in an airport. And she was really interested in the possibilities of scholarly podcasting. We decided to work together and see if we could come up with something specifically that was peer reviewable, because *Witch Please*, for all of its value, was a bit unwieldy to subject to peer review. We put together a grant application with the goal of creating a short run, maybe like five- or six-episode podcast, that would be a good candidate for peer review. The idea was I would record the episodes and we would send them out and I would revise them etc, and then we would post them once they were completed, which is not what ended up happening even a little bit.

What happened is that while Siobhan and I were still in conversations about what this podcast might possibly look like, I just started *Secret Feminist Agenda* for fun, very much in the same sort of impulsive way that I started [another podcast I do called] *Witch Please* with Marcelle [Kosman]. I was new to Vancouver. I was interested in starting to sort of build community. And I was like, 'oh, I have a great idea. I'll start a podcast where I talk to interesting feminists and then I'll have a really great excuse to cold email all of the people in the city I want to meet and I can, like, invite them over and talk to them'. And that was extremely effective. A lot of the early people I interviewed for *Secret Feminist Agenda* are now my friends. So, it was a trap and it worked. What it was for me, was a chance to have conversations with people, to build community, to just talk about ideas, to start to build an intellectual community for myself in this new city and outside of grad school, because that is kind of a weird transition where you go from having this built-in cohort to all of a sudden having to figure out how to build intellectual community for yourself.

And then I was having a conversation with Siobhan one day about what I thought our prototype podcast should be, and Siobhan said, 'Oh, I assumed *Secret Feminist Agenda* is the podcast we were going to use'. And I was like, 'Don't be absurd. That's not scholarly'. And that has been a really interesting locus of my conversations with Siobhan. As an editor, as a scholarly editor, her understanding of scholarship is, in fact, significantly more expansive and flexible than my own. Which is exactly the opposite of what I had always assumed would be true. You hear all of these, you know, 'scholarly editors as gatekeepers', which I think is what functions in some places. But forward-thinking editors are invested in rethinking the forms in which we do our work. But that meant that because I was already making the podcast and it was a weekly podcast, that it was absolutely impossible to do before-the-fact peer review. We were going to have to do cumulative peer review, after-the-fact. We decided that we would structure the podcast into seasons so that they were really sort of distinct cut-off points. And we came up with a sort of, you know, semi-arbitrary definition of a season, which was 15 interviews. And once the season was completed, I would send that to the press. Then the press would begin the peer review process. And because we were already doing this kind of unconventional approach of the after-the-fact peer review, we decided to also make the peer review totally open. The peer reviews are up on the press website. You can read them. You can read my responses to them. The entire process was fundamentally open.

What I think is really key here is that presses understand that you don't need to, and maybe shouldn't, use exactly the same peer review model for every kind of project and every kind of scholarship, because different kinds of scholarship have different kinds of needs in terms of what peer review is doing. For the most part, when you are doing feminist theory your peer reviewers aren't fact checking you. Right? Like, not in the same way that somebody is when their peer reviewing in like a hard science paper where people are checking your methods and going through your data and making sure that you have done things correctly. There they are fact checking you in a much more literal way. Whereas when you do feminist theory, nobody's responding to you and being like, 'nope, you're wrong about feminism'. Instead, people are challenging you, responding to you, expanding the conversation, adding perspectives. It's still this really vital part of how the work operates, of how peer review operates. But, that idea that like 'I will put something out into the world that is incorrect' is less dangerous than, say, if I was writing papers about possible medications that will help save people from COVID-19 and I was just like publishing that shit wherever I wanted to, which is literally happening right now. And so that was really eye-opening for me to realise that this open peer review method works beautifully because the people who are engaging with my scholarship are also feminist media scholars. They were totally ready to embrace the spirit of this project.

Hannah McGregor, Secret Feminist Agenda
and podcast scholar

00:22:47,000 Then when the podcast was finished, I went to the department. I said, 'I want to do a research talk'. Many universities around the world have research talks where faculty members who are actively doing research can present and say, 'hey, here's the research I'm doing'. And usually that is orientated towards ongoing book projects. Maybe ones that are almost finished or ones that are finished. And you present, 'I got this book out or whatever'. So, I did that with the podcast. The podcast was finished, I think, 2015. I went to the department and said, 'I want to do a research talk on the podcast'. I put a research talk together. I said, 'look, here is what represents the original scholarship that's in these podcasts. If these podcasts did not exist, this information, these questions, these ways, and modes of going about this history would not exist if not for this podcast. Thus, this podcast represents a piece of original knowledge or a pursuit of original knowledge'.

And, you know, not many of my colleagues came out. A lot of students did, but not many of my colleagues came out for it, but the ones that were there seemed impressed or whatever, you know, in that venue. And they were like, 'OK, he's putting this stuff out there. We have a chance to interrogate and, you know, all this other stuff'. And so that was well and good. But I wasn't reaching a majority of my colleagues through that way of engaging them.

The next thing I did is I said, 'well, you know, what needs to be done is these things need to be reviewed'. And at the time, the *American Historical Review*, *Journal of American History* and *Public Historian* were all doing reviews of two things, exhibits and digital projects. And to me, this was both. This was an exhibit and a digital project. I sent an email out to the review editors of each of those journals, a pretty long one. And I made the case, 'hey, look, you should review this project'.

Those three journals, the review editors, all three of them initially got back to me and said, 'you're right. Let me get back to you'. Wouldn't commit to reviewing it. Just, 'let me get back to you'. I gave it a couple of months and I returned to those three journals. And *Public Historian* just dropped me altogether, never heard back from the review editor ever. The other two I kept getting, 'you're right' for four years and every four or five months I would, you know, 'hey, where are we on this? You said you get back to me. Haven't heard from you'. And the reply would be, 'you're right. We should review this. Let me get back to you'. And that's where I was for about four years.

And then I went to the Organisation of American Historians meeting. It was in Sacramento in 2019, I think. And there was a session [laughs] by the review editor for the *Journal of American History*. He was on this panel about reviewing digital projects and he said in this panel, 'the greatest hurdle for him as a review editor, is that people do not volunteer their digital projects to be reviewed'. And I just blew up. And the president of the American Historical Association tweeted that quote at the conference and was like, 'hey, I'm in this session. And, you know, the review editor, quote, said this'. And then I went on there, I'm like, 'well, that's really interesting, because for four years I've been asking him to review my digital project and he is only blowing me off. So, I wonder what it takes to actually get noticed'.

And after that tweet, the editor contacted me and said, 'I am actually trying to get this reviewed. The problem is I can't find anybody to review it. And I can't find anybody who thinks they're qualified to review it. And that's why it's not getting reviewed. It's not because I don't want to. It's because I'm missing this element'. And I was like, 'OK, well, let's talk. Maybe I can give you some ideas'.

And then with *Public Historian*, someone I knew who knew the trouble I was going through reached out to the editor, not the review editor, but the editor. And the editor directly contacted me after the meeting and said, 'this is gonna be on fast track. We're going to review this. Don't worry'. And so eventually it did come out. So, I got a review from the *Journal of American History* and I got a review from *Public Historian*. So that was really important for me in this process. It's unfortunate it took four years for it, for me to nag, to get it done, but it did get done and it did come out in 2019.

And so, I needed that to go back to the colleagues who didn't attend the research talk. I had these two reviews, positive reviews. You know, the first sentence of the *Public Historian* said 'this is an extraordinary digital public history project'. Right. And then the other one was a positive review in the *Journal of American History*, the top journal, you know, in my field. And so, I took these two reviews and then I started to go door-to-door, knocking on the door of colleagues who weren't attending my research talk 'hey, how you doing? You know, I got these reviews, I'd like you to read them. Let me send them to you'. And so that was the other phase of this project to convince my colleagues that a project like this merits consideration as a work of original research. And some of them were convinced, others were not. There is this one colleague, when I told them these two journals reviewed this he goes, 'I'd like to read those'. I'm like, 'here you go. Let me know what you think'. And then he came back after he read them and he said, 'I think you are, you know, the epitome of a great teacher and you provide extraordinary service in this department. And I want to thank you'. And I said 'I noticed in the email you didn't say research. So, let's turn round to that because I said this represents original research'. And he goes, 'I don't see it that way', because he's one of these people that thinks research is a book or article.

Robert Cassanello, History of Central Florida

With Voices Present

One of the biggest criticisms regarding the possibility of having a voice present in a podcast is that it stops anonymity, which some say is vital for peer review. I would disagree but do not have the space here to explore the history and solidification of certain forms of review or to comment on the pitfalls of anonymisation of reviewers. Rather it is worth highlighting what the presence of actually being able to hear voices brings to scholarship and the problems it creates beyond review processes.

You can hear excitement; you can hear accents; you can hear inflection; you can hear the identity people bring.

Some of this I find genuinely exciting, such as the ability to feel the thrill of a scholar as they speak, but I am also acutely aware of how certain accents sound 'scholarly' and others do not, closing off doors and ears through prejudice, whether consciously or not.

What does it mean to have voices present in scholarly publishing?

> 00:07:14,000 Coming from the sciences, when I think of academic production, I'm thinking more of completing an experiment, writing it up, putting a poster at a conference, and then actually writing a manuscript. And when I think of that whole process, it is so incredibly slow and for good reason. You do want to make sure that you're being thorough, that your analyses are correct, that you've had peers in your field take a look and recognise that, 'oh, you did this right. But you probably need to alter this thing'… and those are all good things to have, but I think because they're so slow it can really feel tedious at times or just like there's no end in sight. I think people kind of lose their passion or they lose their excitement about a project, and it helps to have interim check-ins that are more uplifting. I think doing a podcast where you get to talk about your work and it's somebody else who doesn't know as much and they're really excited and they're asking all these questions, it's like, 'oh, yeah. What I do is cool'. And it can build that reminder and then you want to continue in that academic process. And so that's where I think it's really useful, especially in the sciences. I mean, you know, you get a piece published, everyone's so excited for you and you're like, 'yeah, I did this work three years ago'.
> **Sadie Witkowski, PhDrinking**

> 00:23:13,000 Sometimes when I'm transcribing I do feel frustrated because they're saying it in a certain way, but my job, when I'm transcribing, is to faithfully

reproduce the words that are said. And sometimes you do miss on that inflexion and how people are talking about things and just the vocal patterns that people have. I also think the accents that people have are an interesting part of this that we rarely talk about. Sometimes someone will say, 'oh, I grew up here', so you'll guess, 'Oh, that's why their accent sounds like this'. But I think it's nice for people to hear people with a wide range of accents talking about math. And of course, I'm not going to put at the top 'this person has a British accent or this person has a Hungarian accent' or whatever. So that's just something that you would only get if you listen to the audio. I do think that's part of what makes it engaging – hearing how people talk and what their voice rises for and what they're really excited about.

Evelyn Lamb, My Favorite Theorem

00:31:44,000 I feel a more personal connection with the voice when I can hear the intonation and inflection of the tone, when someone is saying something and almost hinting at that kind of suggestive nature, which sometimes, especially if you're just glancing through and skimming through a book very fast, you might miss. You might miss that suggestion of sarcasm or hint of irony which is a lot more perceivable within the audio format.

Matt Coward-Gibbs, York Crime Walk and York Death & Culture Walk

00:19:58,000 We wanted to make sure, as much as possible, though we have violated this in a couple of cases, but as much as possible, we wanted to bring in people who had the identity we were discussing. We didn't want white people talking about Black English. I mean, we are already the white people, we need to have someone in the room who is actually black.

Carrie Gillon, The Vocal Fries

00:51:52,000 You can tell a lot about someone from their voice. So you can hear my voice right now. You don't have to see me to know that I'm a white middle class man in all likelihood, and that I'm from America.

And actually, I had a really interesting conversation with someone about this named Vanessa Wells. I was interviewing her for the Africana series. And she is an African-American woman who works on the history of Marxism. I was interviewing her about women, African-American women Marxists. We were talking about the extent to which she's herself committed to Marxism. And I said, 'are you interested in getting a history of Marxism right? Or are you interested in making a case for Marxism?' And she said, 'both'. And I said, 'oh, that's really interesting, because as a historian of philosophy, I'm usually totally neutral and uncommitted'.

And then she made an interesting point, later on in the conversation, because we were talking about voice, like the voice that you hear in the podcast. And she said, 'you know, that thing, that pose that you adopt, where you're just the neutral historian, sort of godlike historian of philosophy', like "here's how it was", is something that a woman of colour probably just couldn't get away with doing. Because people would be like, "oh, what's your angle?"'. Or they wouldn't give her the authority to do that. They would think of her as sort of coded by her voice in a very specific way. They might like that, they might want to listen to her because she's an African-American woman even, but she doesn't have the luxury of having a voice, that means nothing.

And my voice really means nothing, which is to say that it means something. Namely, it's the default. It's the voice of authority. It's the voice of 'you can trust me'. 'He sounds like he knows what he's talking about'. 'His grammar is always right'. 'He's not saying gettin'. He's saying getting. He's not saying ain't'. 'He's like talking in a very rhetorically elevated way. But he's also not talking in a way that marks the speech in any way as belonging to a certain type of person'.

And I think that really made me think of the idea that I had this privilege. People talk about white privilege these days, and that is a great example because literally something that I can do as a podcaster and you could do as well, although you have this northern accent, so if you did a podcast in the history of philosophy, people would literally think, 'oh, this is kind of cute', whereas I when I do it, they're just like, 'oh, like generic American male voice. Fine'. So, they don't even think about who it is. That's my point.

Peter Adamson, History of Philosophy
without Any Gaps

00:44:31,000 I've not thought about that too much. I think my voice probably reveals my education level. And I would suspect it might reveal some of my origin. I did grow up in Indiana. They've got an accent. The stereotypical Southern accent in America is like, 'hey, y'all. Indiana'. Their version is called the Hoosier Accent. And there are times in my life when I still speak like a Hoosier. And I think that could probably be identified. But Indiana is primarily white folks. So, I would suspect that if someone heard my podcast, they would take me just as a decently educated white person, which is funny to think about as a person of colour who is queer.

Ezra Mattaridi, STEMS and Leaves

00:42:54,000 Even in the podcast episodes that I record, there will be people who talk over me. And you can listen to the podcast episodes, and perhaps it's a biased view, but this is feedback we also received about how the podcast sounds to people who listen to it. So I think that there's something there that needs to be said about it. Like, it's not that it's specific to academic podcasting as such, but I do think women's voices do get erased, whether it's guests, whether it's a host, whether it's anybody else. It is a fairly gendered space and masculinity plays out in weird ways. I guess it's a certain sort of academic authority that needs to be portrayed and it gets portrayed in a very gendered way.

You can have a podcast that you put up on the Internet and all of those things. The barriers to entry are not very high, but the barriers to actually being able to reach a wider audience are pretty significant because they're mediated by your traditional structures. What makes a good media voice? Why is it that you have to speak a certain kind of English? Fortunately, in podcasting you don't have to look any particular way, but you have to sound a particular way. You have to be able to command that kind of authority in speaking about the subject that you do.

Sarayu Natarajan, Ganatantra

A Mode of Knowledge Creation

Data Collection

A few years back, I undertook some research on environmental injustices in an alumna (ex)factory town with a massive red mud storage facility and problems with toxic waste. The research team included another anthropologist, a chemist, and an investigative journalist. Aside from interviewing local residents, activists, and local politicians with my notebook in hand, I went back and interviewed some of the same people again with a mic. I also interviewed my co-researchers. Here the podcast creation process was also a form of research, partly because I got different data when I asked the same questions with and without the mic (both from my interlocutors and those in the team).

Of course, it's easy for me to think of ways to collect data in my discipline or adjacent disciplines, but there are plenty of other ways in which podcasting can be a form of data collection, especially when sound or talking is central to the research. Sometimes it's because people are not willing to give their time for a research interview, but will for a podcast because it gives them a platform for their expertise or they see a benefit of having a certain viewpoint more widely disseminated. But even talking to other scholars (or oneself) can be data collection as it allows the development of theoretical or conceptual nuance and depth.

In what ways can podcasting be data collection?

> 00:04:25,000 The podcast in the right circumstances can become the research. So, it is an actual research outcome. It's not just showcasing research. It is synthesising research. And that marries well with my long practice of doing crafted audio storytelling and oral history. I've always been concerned with the orality of oral history and trying to convey that and have always rebelled against that earlier tendency of oral historians to work off the dreaded transcript, which is just heresy to me. I mean, all the meaning that you lose in that.
>
> **Siobhan McHugh, documentary podcaster maker and podcast scholar**

> 00:21:50,000 Most of the time most people like to be interviewed, but we realised that they even appreciate it more if the interview is made public, recorded, and made available. Because I think it's acknowledging and recognising, 'OK, he's an expert', 'he or she has something to say'.
>
> In the end, you may generate data as well, both are interviews for your research and for a podcast. But the podcast, the fact that that is public, it's online, I think this adds value.
>
> **Emanuele Fantini, The Sources of the Nile**

00:14:40,000 It's data collection, but it's also dissemination. Since I'm open about it, I will do research about this, but I will also distribute it widely. I'm aware that there are some things that might not be shared with me, that could be shared. On the other hand, what was really interesting to see was that people are more willing to participate in this kind of research than the traditional way of doing research, because as I told you, I did double research at one point. And the ones that were participating in the traditional one, they didn't have time for me, I had to really negotiate with them to give me that one-hour time while these other ones, of course, I was kind of familiar with them as well, they were like, 'oh, lovely, come, you can stay at our house for the night if you want to'. I think it's something about the openness and giving meaning to something more than just that closed academic community that creates meaning also to those that are participating.

**Maria Ehrnström-Fuentes, Världar i Omställning/
Worlds in Transition**

00:12:04,000 I've been working on a book project for a few years. And the book project has been one of these on again, off again things, because there's been other things, other projects I've been involved with, other things I've had to write. The book project was always going to be about this thing with the Left, these intra-left debates and working on this show, in a sense, has become a kind of a data gathering exercise for me in a way, because it's just this ability to talk to people, to set up the questions for them. First of all, to have to read some of their work, but then when you edit their words, when you figure out the logical sequence in which to present their ideas, it's in that careful editing where you're trying to find the parts that bring their authentic message out most completely for the audience, perhaps having to re-record a question because the answer didn't quite fit the original question that you had intended. With all of this you just get a much greater sense of how people are actually thinking. Sometimes it's not as alive for you if all you're doing is reading the dusty books. You know, the arcane academic tomes don't quite have as much vibrancy.

Nicholas Kiersey, Fully Automated

00:16:01,000 I'm stressing or emphasising talking to myself [as a means of gathering data] so much because I have this setting using headphones. Every time I recorded anything [for Podlog], I used headphones and it was very important for me to use headphones with a microphone and direct monitoring so I could hear myself talking to myself. My voice appears in the middle of my head. This technological mediation is really what does the trick. It is an intimate way to talk to yourself in a way you'd never have the chance to talk to yourself, really, without technology.

These soliloquies develop their own structure and this is what became very fascinating to me because, for example, stumbling over your words and being unsatisfied with the way you can express yourself at one moment and then coming up with some word, trying out this like you try on pants or try on new shoes, and then you walk in those new shoes for a bit, and then and then it feels better, it feels adequate, and you try it out in your mouth and in your ears, and later on, you come upon those same words and you have no written text, so you don't know what you were talking about, but even the sound of those words, you were trying like days or weeks before, remind you of those ideas and then you have some kind of a link back to those ideas. And then you remember what you were talking about and you have connections. And so, yes this is kind of a non-linear process that is hidden in the linear one.

Moritz Klenk, Podlog

Tool for Thinking

I don't like Auguste Rodin's sculpture *The Thinker*. It depicts a man bent over, chin on his hand, staring at the floor. What a terrible way to think. Is that how you think? I think best with my feet out in the world, in conversation with myself and others, and with my mouth, body, ears, and mind open.

Scholarly podcasting can be sensemaking through conversation; it can push scholars to change their preferred register of explanation and pull podcasters into reading and listening about topics, themes, and ideas that they would not usually, forging connections between seemingly unrelated ideas and improving their thinking and scholarship.

How does podcasting help you think?

> 00:08:54,000 My interest in podcasting was this free-flow style of sensemaking together as the conversation moves. I didn't know that, to be honest, upfront. So I really prepared and sent them a list of questions, but I very quickly observed my own interview style being more this free-flowing sensemaking way.
>
> **Corina Enache, The Human Show**

> 00:32:50,000 It's true, mathematicians love a blackboard. You know, we'll start writing on a blackboard and drawing, but if you don't have that, you have to really begin to think about what it is you're trying to explain and how you can say the words to convey that sentiment to someone. I think it's an interesting exercise for mathematicians to actually proceed this way.
>
> **Kevin Knudson, My Favorite Theorem**

> 00:18:24,000 So I work on a few viruses. I mean, I spent most of my career working on polio virus. One virus. And then we diversified a few years ago. And I mainly just read about polio virus, very few other

viruses, because it was my feeling that I didn't understand, and I didn't know enough. But on the podcast,
on TWIV [*This Week in Virology*], we cover all viruses,
not just mine or the other hosts'. And so, I have been
reading now for 12 years papers on basically every
virus out there. When I go to a meeting to do a podcast, I have to read all about the four or five guests,
what they've been doing. And if I go to a university, I
do the same thing. So, I've enormously broadened my
knowledge of virology to the point where when we
write new editions of our textbook, it's always me…
and when I want to see what's new in the field for the
next version of the textbook, I look at my podcast
episodes because there I'm covering what I think is
really interesting and broadly applicable. But that's
just virology.

So it makes me think broadly about my own viruses when I'm trying to solve problems. It gives me
experimental breadth because I see techniques that I
wouldn't have encountered, probably. But then I do
podcasts in microbiology, evolution, parasitism, neu-
roscience, immunology. So I'm reading in those fields,
which I would never [normally do]. And you get to
learn other approaches and you find that many of
these fields actually have a lot in common. But you
can also see the unique aspects and you can apply that
to your work. You can apply experimental techniques
and approaches.

This Week in Evolution covers really all organisms,
not just viruses and bacteria, but, you know, mammals
and birds and reptiles, insects, everything, plants. And
boy, does that give you breadth to really think about
how things evolved and how they relate to each other.

An example is, I've been going to these giant virus
meetings for the past few years in Germany. These are
spurred by the finding that you can get these really big,
big, big viruses that we've never seen before. And they
have a unique biology. The people who study them are

really interested in ecology. I never thought about ecology. Never. But now I thought about it enough so that this year I introduced a new ecology lecture into my course and the next textbook edition is going to have an ecology chapter because it's all about how viruses interact not just with their hosts, but with everything else in the environment. This is so important and it was not something I ever appreciated. And I ascribe it to the podcast because I got invited to these meetings to do podcasts and that's what turned me on to it.

Vincent Racaniello, This Week in Virology

00:37:31,000 And I think that's the thing, it's like I listen to anything that catches my eye on NBN [*New Books Network*] because, yeah, I'm not going to read it, but I'll spend an hour listening to that. And there might be some crossover. And actually, there might be an interesting crossover I've never thought of. I think it opens up those disciplinary boundaries. Podcasting academia for me makes us all more interdisciplinary. And that is not a bad thing in my eyes.

I think, in a sense, it has bled into my scholarly practise because I listened to these podcasts and I draw on them. It helps to make those connections… even if you're not actively understanding, you're not actively incorporating that into your work, it does sit with you, and it therefore does bleed in, as it were, because we're not putting up these plastic barriers, but there's almost this kind of collegiate osmosis that's going on around everything that we listen to, read, see, hear etc etc.

Matt Coward-Gibbs, York Crime Walk and
York Death & Culture Walk

Part of a Process

Because I always underestimate how long things take, and because I get distracted by new ideas, I'm not so great at finishing off the projects I started. I spent years and years of my life researching urban change in a small city in India, but I hardly published any of it. That's what you get for following your curiosity. But now that I've finished this book on podcasting, I want to revisit the topic, do some follow-up research, and get into the latest research on urban India. And so I think I'll try to start a podcast on the topic. I don't know what else it'll lead to, maybe some journal articles, maybe a book about door-to-door salesmen, but I know that a podcast will help me get there.

I think it's a mistake to think about different mediums as somehow distinct or as the end of a project as an output. An intellectual inquiry is a process that doesn't start or end with a publication, it's a multimodal series of processes that keeps on going until you – or others – decide it should stop. A podcast episode could be the spark of an idea that becomes a paper, a way of thinking through ideas or searching for a new point of view, a way to explore a topic without upsetting a journal that wants to be the first to publish a dataset or, once something is published, a way for a new cycle of reflection to begin.

How does podcasting fit into wider processes of scholarly inquiry?

> 00:21:43,000 We sort of work out ideas that might eventually become a paper or a chapter or a book or whatever. And we sort of think through our ideas in conversation with each other, which we might do anyway, whether or not we were doing a podcast.
> **Anindya Raychaudhuri, State of the Theory Podcast**

> 00:23:30,000 I was thinking about it this morning because I'm trying to write something at the moment about overseas enfranchisement and I've radically changed my opinion about what that's about. But it's not that I've changed my opinion, I think that what you see in the podcast when we talk about the issue, is our ways of actually trying to muddle through what's

actually going on. It's quite a complex landscape and we're trying to muddle through what the possible explanations might be.

We had a conversation in 2017 about the overseas vote. We have another one in 2018. We had another one again when the last general election happened. And I can see that, you know, slowly, slowly, we're peeling back the layers of the analysis. Now, you wouldn't necessarily make any of that visible in a journal article, which is the traditional form that I am now trying to write in, but it wouldn't be possible to get to that journal article without having had those discussions first. And I say discussions because I think that very often, we sit on our desk and we trouble through things ourselves and we write and we edit and produce polished text. And actually, there is something about that process of discussion that helps you with the analysis.

And I'm very much of the opinion that even when a journal article is written by one person, it's actually produced in dialogue as a community of scholars, whether those are people you've actually spoken to or whether they're just people who appear on the page. For me, it's not exactly miss-turns, it's more a showing of that process of knowledge production. Are we producing academic knowledge? I think we definitely are producing academic knowledge. It might not be the academic knowledge that we would commit to a journal article or monograph, but they're steps on the way.

Michaela Benson, Brexit Brits Abroad

00:03:50,000 I did this research project on small company markets in London. I went round and interviewed a bunch of old men. There should be a particular word for oral histories collected from old men in armchairs, buffer-o-graphy or something like that, I dunno, I've had years of practice listening to my dad. I got this really quite extensive collection of oral histories.

There's this sense that we're obliged to try and get this stuff into high-ranking journals and so forth, and, you know, that takes years. I've written a paper with a colleague on the 'silent legitimacies of material structures' or something, it's all really dry. And it might end up in some horribly kind of bowdlerised form in a journal in a couple of years' time with just one of those data tables that tells nobody anything.

But still, I've got this interesting story that I can't sabotage my basic job-related outputs by publishing it. I published it as a narrative report for the practitioner audience so they could download it, but still, I thought this is a hybrid thing that I could do to try and communicate some of this financial history as an accessible document that people might be interested in, and not at the same time sabotage those research outputs in the way that trying to write a Penguin or something, a piece of popular financial history, might do.

So it was quite emergent, but I had these two structures in my mind from the very beginning. One of which is the narrative arc of the undergraduate course that I've been teaching for a decade and the other is this historical narrative that begins in the open outcry markets of London in the '60s and really goes through to about 2010. It's quite a specific historical narrative. The reason I knew about these markets is that in my twenties, when I first graduated, I worked as a finance journalist in this area. There was a sort of autobiographical element as well, and I wanted to mess around with the way that they could be tied up together and made into something, but without the capacity of writing a book, without being commissioned to write a book or having the time to do so. I thought it would be a way of chipping away at these narratives and these stories that I wanted to tell. I always conceived of it as a project in itself.

Philip Roscoe, How to Build a Stock Exchange:
Making Finance Fit for the Future

00:34:03,000 There is a way in which the podcast is an unfinished form. It's a type of thought experiment. Or a draft conversation, if you will. I know from talking with people after we turn off the tape that the conversations about their current work, and even sometimes about the work that's already published, is generative.

Most of the time, I'd say 80 percent of the time, once we cut the tape and end the conversation, we have a little chit chat goodbye at the end and many people would say, 'that was really useful. I really started to think about things in ways that I hadn't before. Those were really good questions. Thank you for reading so closely'.

It's generative because it's a bit like having a workshop or a work-in-progress seminar between three people. I mean, it's just a small group of people, but it's people who are thoughtfully engaging and who can make connections between your work and other work. We're doing a podcast every week, we're digesting a lot of material and creating a set of synapses and networks of connections between all these different works that's fairly unique.

Cymene Howe, Cultures of Energy

00:19:51,000 The fourth episode was on the struggle for land reform in Brazil, that's a big thing, too. And it was with this anthropologist and a farmer that she worked with for a long time. And he now has his piece of land, but for many years, he was in the public fight for his own land. And after the episode came out, he sent it to the mayor. That was so interesting, you know, and he sent the episode to the mayor and to the chamber of deputies from the city. And the mayor was like, 'wow, this really helps make our municipality more visible. Now, I understand what you guys are doing. All the research you were doing together with this anthropologist'.

This way the podcast travels back into the community. Because we do our articles and books and they go back to the community, of course. But I mean something like an audio material that can be spread so easily and can be listened to so easily and for a few minutes. I think it's a kind of return, and also starting a new cycle of reflection or insights or thinking about that community or whatever they're talking about. There's another cycle of knowledge that starts again. That's very interesting, I think, and it only works well because this farmer was on the programme, not only the anthropologist that was working with them and talking about the research, but he was there talking about it with her.

Soraya Fleischer, Mundaréu

4 How? With Craft

Scholarly podcasting is a craft which, when done well, builds on an appreciation of the medium, thrives when changing academic structures and is formed by words and other sounds. In this third part of the book, I go through the steps needed to make a scholarly podcast, drawing on my own teaching experience and, primarily, the thoughts of the podcasters I interviewed. These words are meant particularly for students, teachers, researchers, and others who have no prior background in audio or podcasting and want to start turning their ideas into podcasts; I will not dive deeply into technical specifics because a printed book is not the best place to do this and, to be frank, there are much better qualified people than me to do so. Much of my thinking about how to teach podcasting to scholars, including students, comes from working together with Dumitriţa Holdiş when we taught workshops both at our home institution, Central European University, and for NGO staff, journalists, and scholars at other universities across Europe. The insights from the podcasters I spoke with should be of interest to all, even those already with considerable experience with podcasting.

There are exercises throughout this chapter, pedagogical suggestions in most sections, and an additional resource in the annex.

DOI: 10.4324/9781003006596-4

What should scholars think about before they embark on podcast making?

00:42:07,000 It does require an engagement with the craft of podcasting. We've all been to conferences where people just stare down at the text of their conference paper and read it as fast as possible, trying not to trip for 30 minutes and then, you know, raise their eyes and look out at the audience that offers a very polite smattering of applause, and they sit down. That approach is bad in an academic conference setting, but it's 100 times worse in a podcast setting, because you have no physicality, you have no eye contact. It's much easier to leave a podcast than it is to leave a conference room.

It's not super complicated to think about. The first thing I would start with is narrative. OK, so you want to talk about something today. You want to talk about CRISPR gene technology. You need to think of a human story that imparts that information about CRISPR that you want to impart. The other thing that you have to bear in mind is this idea of contingency and frameworks. That people don't want to be hectored. They don't want to be told that they're ignorant. They don't want to be bullied into thinking a particular way. They want to authentically engage with material. And that requires presenting it with a lot of latitude.

Martin Spinelli, podcast scholar

00:42:03,000 It doesn't just organically happen, it actually involves either prep in terms of working out your story points and then post-production in terms of editing, and the ability of people to actually be energised and live and all the rest of it. It just doesn't happen by itself. And it takes a huge amount of time. Audio podcasting's dirty secret is that audio storytelling takes tonnes of time.

Siobhan McHugh, documentary podcaster
maker and podcast scholar

00:31:30,000 OK, so the whole thing, including preparation. Reading a book usually takes a couple of days. I would say reading a book is 13, 14 hours, if it's a regular sized book. Then writing the interview takes about two hours. Sitting down and writing out the questions takes about two hours. The interviews are almost always 60 minutes. Editing it takes two to three times as long as the interview itself. So, a 60-minute interview takes about two to three hours to edit the audio. Going through and removing pauses and weird things and, sometimes, my own mistakes.

And then post-editing. I have to make a YouTube video out of it for older people that don't know how to use podcasting. I create all the art for it. I do the photography, all the pictures of my guests after the interview. I'll tell them, 'pretend like you're talking to me. I'm gonna go over here and take your picture and you look over where I was sitting and pretend you're talking and I'll take your picture'. I edit those photos and create art and create all the promo stuff. There's this great software that makes like a little audio and picture with transcript. That usually takes about an hour. They found that when you do subtitles, people are twice as likely to turn the sound on a video. And then I create the blog post for it.

And the other big thing is every single episode has a transcript. We do full transcripts. And this is really important to me because, number one, accessibility. I want anyone to be able to enjoy this. And, secondly, people in classrooms have found it useful because not all their students want to listen to something, but they might read something. Professors have found the transcripts really useful. And then, thirdly, bloggers love a transcript because if they want to blog about something in an episode, what a pain in the ass it is to have to find, 'Oh, where did they talk about that one thing? I don't remember where that was at'. But if they've got a transcript, they can just do a search for the word, and boom, there it is.

Blair Hodges, The Maxwell Institute Podcast

01:00:28,000 The gentleman is the person who knows how to play the bagpipes and doesn't. And maybe, you know, the best podcast person is the amateur, who knows they could make a podcast, but they don't inflict it on us. On the one hand, I'm very pro the democratisation that podcasting affords. But on the other hand, I think we need to show respect for the medium and respect for the principles of audio storytelling and the grammar and logic of sound. And I would like to see all of these factors properly analysed and recognised in the academy via scholarly writing and perhaps via podcasts.

Siobhan McHugh, documentary podcaster maker and podcast scholar

Create (an idea for podcasting)

Podcasting, like any medium, lends itself to certain forms. There are no hard and fast rules; podcasting thrives on the innovation engendered by digital scholarship. However, at every turn you should ask yourself, 'is this an idea that suits podcasting?' Are you expressing the idea in a way that suits the medium? Would it be better as a book? An infographic? Does it only have to be one thing, or can it be more than one (like this book with the accompanying audio)?

Many scholars and students are good at expressing themselves through text (though many are terrible in spite of, or maybe because of, spending decades in academia). It is, after all, what most of us are primarily trained to do. We learn to organise the information in a certain way so as best to present it to our audience – usually our colleagues or teachers or peers. Audio works differently. A good graph can be extremely useful to help understand a complex research topic, but try explaining that graph over the phone. Likewise, you might be able to capture the emotion in a guest's voice on a podcast, but unless you are a skilled writer, you might struggle to convey the depth and subtleties of that emotion.

Example no 1. You have a brilliant piece of research you want to communicate to the world. You've just 'given a paper' on this topic. You want to record yourself reading out this paper and put it online. STOP. Ask yourself, 'would anyone listen?' (I mean anyone who would not anyway read the paper). It will be really hard to find an audience for a single episode, never mind a single episode which consists of a person reading out a paper. Rather, you need to work out if the topic justifies a podcast series. Maybe the paper you wrote can be the background you need to create a podcast series, in which you discuss emerging research with fellow experts in the field. Such a podcast will allow you to think through new ideas as they develop and to create a network with fellow scholars.

Example no 2. You have just got some funding to start a new project. Great, you think, 'let's have a podcast in which I showcase my expertise in the field and put it up on the project website. I'll call the podcast the name of the project to promote it'. STOP. Ask yourself, 'have you ever cared about anyone else's project as a project?' (I mean, you might be interested in the research or even the researcher, but the actual project?!) Nobody wants to listen to self-promotion or project promotion. There's way too much of that in academia. Don't inflate your (fragile) ego, rather see this as a great opportunity to use the project money you have received to collaborate with scholars who have podcasting skills, to create a series on the topic (but not about the project), and build a community of listeners over time that, if you do it right, will outlive your project.

Example no 3. You're organising a conference/workshop/seminar series. 'Let's make a podcast series out of it', you say to yourself. 'We can record all the talks and put them up online.' STOP. Ask yourself, 'are conference presentations always the most interesting things to listen to?'

(I mean, the research might be great, but often you learn more about it talking to the presenter over coffee). Why not see if the conference budget extends to hiring a PhD student who could create a brilliant new podcast series based on excerpts from the talk combined with in-depth discussions with the researchers the day before or after. It would make for a much more dynamic series and allow a student to network with people in their field.

Example no 4. You're a student who is really into a particular topic. You're going to write your dissertation/ thesis on it. You could imagine working on that topic in the future. You decide to create an audio version of your final work. STOP. Ask yourself, 'are you creating yourself a lot of extra work for little reward?' (I mean, unless you have a department which is open-minded towards multi-modal scholarship, you might be getting yourself nothing more than a pat on the back). Why not think beyond the confines of your dissertation? Maybe start a podcast series on a related topic, use it to interview people who work in the field, and then at the end of your enrolment as a student create an audio documentary by taking excerpts from all your past interviews and combining them with a script you write. You can also continue your podcast once you graduate.

Example no 5. You're a teacher and you want to use podcasts in your teaching. GREAT. Here are some ideas of how podcasting can be integrated into your course (and I'll mention more about teaching in the following sections). Many teachers replace – or give students the option to replace – a written assignment with an audio assignment. I've done this in my own classes and worked together with other teachers to help them do this. I've put an example of this type of assignment in the annex. It's designed for the social sciences and humanities but can be adapted. If you have a class that allows it, such as oral history, then embedding a group podcast assignment in the whole course could work as a way of creating public-facing collaborative content together with the students (see *A History of Central*

Florida). Podcasts as assignments are great because students invest more effort into their work. In part, this is because it's not only their teachers but also their peers, family, and others who might hear the final result. Learning a new skill like podcasting alongside the course content is a great way to reinforce what's being learnt because thinking through questions, arranging interviews with guests, and then editing conversations pushes the students to have deep engagements with ideas. Moreover, at some point or other, many students learn the ability to knock out an essay with little effort, but unless they already have prior audio skills, they will struggle to do so with a podcast, leading to a more considered approach to their assignments.

You can record your lectures or interviews you make with other experts and make them available online for students (or a wider public). Another possibility is to have students interview you or a guest speaker after the class and make a podcast that they can then upload to the e-learning platform or elsewhere. This pushes students to create questions related to the topic of the class, facilitating engagement with the content both during and after the session. I am relatively new to teaching and found that having to sit down for a 20-minute conversation after 100 minutes of teaching was hard on my brain (so now I would only recommend my students do it with guest lecturers!). A variation of this idea is to record your lectures and have students edit them down to create shorter versions. If they are good, you can then use these podcasts for next year's teaching. Another course-based option is to have students record a group discussion about each class. It pushes them to distil what they think are the most important ideas in what you're teaching. You can combine this with you being interviewed post-class or students using segments of your lecture as described above. You can also pre-record lectures and ask students to listen to them before class. This frees up class time for other activities. If you do this, then try to keep your lectures to no more than 15 minutes (or in 15-minute blocks) and ask your students to listen to the podcasts without getting distracted by the busyness of phone or computer screens.

What tips do seasoned pros have for those thinking about creating a new podcast?

00:52:36,000 The first thing people ask is, 'what kind of microphones do I need to buy?' 'OK, hold on a second. Let's talk about what kind of show you want to make first, like what your goals are, before we jump there'.

Jenna Spinelle, Democracy Works

00:52:50,000 If I were to offer some tips to academics who are thinking about launching a podcast, I would encourage them to first figure out who their audience is. Second, I would encourage them to understand the unique characteristics of podcasting as a different audio medium. And third, I would say don't spend a lot of time trying to get conventional academic structures to 'respect' the work you do in your podcast, because those two spheres, those two fields, feel at odds to me. Think about it as serving a different purpose. Whether it's a personal purpose, whether it's a promotional purpose, whether it's a social purpose, a space for you and other colleagues to have as your own and share. All of those things are good and valuable.

Martin Spinelli, podcast scholar

00:09:07,000 And you have to think, well, 'what am I trying to do? What am I trying to communicate here? And what's my medium? My medium is audio. My medium is podcasting. How are people listening? What are they listening on? Where are they listening? How's it going to fit into their day? And what am I trying to do really? And what are my tools?' Your tools when you're writing a journal article are words, referencing and maybe images. If you move that online and there are digital academic platforms, and obviously when you blog, you can hyperlink and you can add video and embed things. When you think about academic podcasting, I think you've got to think about the medium. And that might mean bits of drama, it might mean getting somebody to voice up some quotes or using music or to use scripting. You've got to appreciate the medium.

Richard Berry, podcast scholar

00:01:16,000 It's all the basic stuff, starting with the core idea: your niche in the market. What are you offering that other people aren't offering? Because as we all know, there are so many podcasts out there. Think about having a niche name. As you know '*The Panpsycast*' – a lot of people just don't know how to pronounce the name of the show or people don't know how to spell it. I think that's cool because it creates a sense of identity, but also it means you can find it. And have an eye-catching logo. These are the basic things you need to do before you do anything else.

Jack Symes, The Panpsycast

00:26:29,000 I think people, like a lot of the time, particularly academics, they project a set of values inherited from the world of scholarly publishing onto their podcast endeavours fruitlessly, pointlessly. Why would we need to do that? You know, the journal article is one mode of expression. Podcasting is another. They're going to do two very, very different things and they're going to engage with the world in two very, very different ways. It would be as foolish to try and tick all those boxes that you tick in a lot of high-profile academic journal article publishing, as it would be to try and write an academic article in the most breezy and unedited, speculative, fluid, reflexive way possible.

Martin Spinelli, podcast scholar

Exercise 1 Developing an Idea for a New Podcast Series

Please have a think about a podcast series you would like to create and answer the following prompts.
Series title:
First Episode topic:
Podcast Concept: (internal note detailing what you want to do and why it's suited to podcasting rather than other forms of communication)
Description – series and episodes: (the short public text that will accompany the podcast online)
Audience and dissemination: (who will listen – academics, another specialised community, your students, etc. How will you find them and get them to listen to your podcast?)

Listen (to loads of podcasts)

You definitely, probably, hopefully listen to a lot of podcasts already. Otherwise, why would you want to make one? But do you listen closely? It is extremely useful to close-listen to different types of podcasts. A lot of the nuances of communication may be discipline specific, for instance, in contemporary anthropology we rightly think a lot about representation of the 'other' due to our colonial history of studying 'exotic people' in 'exotic places' that we are yet to come completely to terms with. Putting such discipline-specific conversations to one side, a good practical and general starting point is to think about communication in terms of clarity of structure, i.e. the order in which things happen in a podcast. A useful exercise is listening to a podcast whilst taking notes about what's happening, how it's happening, and for how long it's happening (see Exercise 2 below).

If you're teaching a course, then having podcasts in your syllabi is a great idea. Depending on the course level, relevance, and academic depth of the podcast, it might be useful to set the students' questions to keep in mind when listening to a particular episode. This is not only useful for guiding students towards particularly relevant sections but might also help focus the students if they are listening on the bus, whilst looking after kids, cleaning the house, or at work, etc.

Exercise 2 Structured Listening

Choose a few podcasts and analyse their structure. Choose ones related to the type of podcast you'd like to make, but also ones that you think are well made. Listen to the podcasts carefully, and make notes using the below schemata:

Minutes	Broad segment structure e.g. intro, main section, outro	What is the content? i.e. what is being told or asked or conveyed (think about the sequential ordering of the content) e.g. 1. overview of the writing of the Indian constitution, 2. question about the uniform civil code, 3. argument about its politicisation	How is it happening? e.g. group discussion, narration, readings, interviews, music, sound

Please also think about the following questions:
What was the topic(s) of the podcast?
Who was the audience?
Can you describe or draw the structure of the podcast narrative?

Structure (the elements of your show)

What possible elements might you have in a podcast? There are six broad categories that most content falls into.

Narration: Scripted or freestyle talking by the host(s). Often used to give context & analysis, to guide the listener, or to link various segments together with narrative flow.

Interview: With a guest or guests either in the studio, online, or in the field.

Group Discussion: A different dynamic than interviews, though still usually led by the host(s).

Readings: Actors or the host reading materials such as books, letters, or diaries.

Sounds: Recordings of ambient sound, sonic phenomena, soundscapes, news cuttings, archival materials, etc.

Music: Songs or instrumental pieces that either directly relate or pass comment upon the topic (different from background music).

Different content lends itself to certain elements, i.e. history works great in narrative form which is why there are so many 'A History Of…' podcast series. But before you decide on what elements you'd like in your podcast have a serious think – and even do some serious experiments – about how best to convey content. There are countless academic podcasts that consist of discussions between two scholars in which one scholar asks the other questions about their work (I've made lots of them and I like both making them and listening to them). You may wish to make another podcast in this form – there's nothing wrong with this – but also think if you could potentially try something different and, if you don't, if you'll be able to find an audience in a very crowded field.

It's one thing to know what elements you want in your podcast, but you also need to decide how you will order it. As such, it's really helpful to sit down and map out the broad structure of your first episode before you start recording (see Exercise 3). If you are a teacher asking students to make a podcast then you can either set what elements are going to be in the podcast, as I have done in the sample assignment, or have the students choose it themselves.

How do scholars structure their podcasts?

00:07:24,000 I was thinking about the audio medium. And because in a written format you can always, as a reader, refer back, which you're not able to do as easily in an audio format, I was thinking, 'well this probably needs to have some kind of clear structure'.

There are other podcasts that do segments, sort of re-curring segments. Every single episode will contain some of these segments and most of these segments act as a sort of structuring device. I ran this past my colleagues at [The University of] Sheffield and then whenever we were preparing to do an episode, I also ran past the outline to the person who was due to be interviewed. And in the end, we settled on a structure that basically starts with a segment called 'Explain This to Me Like I'm Five Years Old'... And doing this at the beginning of the podcast I feel also, to some degree, sets the tone for the rest of it.

And then something else that we try to end on is something convivial, something hopeful at the end of a podcast, which comes from *The Good Place*, the podcast based on the NBC television show *The Good Place*, which always ends on something good. And I thought that was a nice way to end things. So that's also the final segment.

Judith Krauss, The Convivial Conservation Podcast

00:06:58,000 I would say about 20 episodes ago, maybe 20, probably halfway through the podcast, I decided that I need to start off with an introduction of 'Core Takeaways', which is the simplest way that I can think of explaining the most important things of what I'm going to say. For anyone that doesn't care about the scientific details, that is going to be something like a core takeaway for them that is interesting and that they can understand, and then I say, 'now let's get into the scientific details'. So, for anyone else that wants that information, they'll have it.

Stephanie Caligiuri, The People's Scientist

00:29:46,000 People started listening from the very beginning and they started writing in questions. And early on I said, 'let's read these questions as part of the episode. It'll be great content and engages the listener at the same time', which I think is really essential. A lot of podcasts don't do that, but I think it's a mistake. I think you're leaving information on the table.

Vincent Racaniello, This Week in Virology

00:08:27,000 We didn't think, 'OK, we have to have a banter segment', but we thought we had to have some kind of an introduction. What happened over time was that the introduction became a kind of counterbalance to the work of the interview. At some point, a few people began writing to us to say, 'you know, I really just listen to the first segment'. It seems like it's not really the point. I guess that's kind of a nice thing to hear. Perhaps it's because the introduction offers an intimate glimpse into somebody's life. What's going through your mind that day? What's happened in the past couple of days? Funny stories. And I think we tried to approach it with levity for the most part, because a lot of the content of the interviews is quite heavy. I mean, we're talking about climate change. We're talking about the Anthropocene and Capitalocene. We're talking about species extinction. It's important material, but it's heavy stuff and we've come to feel that the climate communication, because it often works these heavy emotions, can be very overwhelming. It can lead to situations where people turn off from the topic because they just can't handle it emotionally. It's completely understandable. So, by interspersing some lightness and even some joy into this topic, the idea was to create a more emotionally textured landscape with points of refuge and relief. Even if, yes, the podcast takes on a lot of topics that everyone should reasonably feel very concerned about.

Dominic Boyer, Cultures of Energy

Exercise 3 Structuring Your Elements

Please fill in this table. Whilst you will probably not plan every podcast in such detail, it is an extremely useful exercise when thinking through your first show(s) if you are not used to working with audio.

Time	Segments	Content Element	Transition element	Background sound/music/silence
start from 0 and count the minutes to give you an idea of how long your podcast will be e.g. 0–4 (4), 5–7 (2), 8–14 (6). Podcasts can be of any length	the broad structure of your episode e.g. intro, topic 1, news, listeners' correspondence, outro – or context, analysis, reflection. Note: one segment may contain multiple types of 'content elements'	this will depend on the format of your podcast and the type of material you are able to collect. Some podcasts have a format dominated by a single content element (e.g. an interview with an author about their book or a group discussion on a certain topic), whilst others utilise a greater mix of different elements	e.g. jingle, sound, music. Note: not all podcasts use transitions, especially those framed by more scholarly concerns	note: your choices matter a lot in terms of tone and pace – i.e. the feeling it helps create

(Continued)

Narration	Interview	Group Discussion	Readings	Sounds	Music
Scripted or freestyle talking by the host(s). Often used to give context & analysis, to guide the listener, or to link various segments together with narrative flow	With guest or guests either in the studio, via a VOIP or in the field. Audio/radio documentaries will often move between 'cuts' and the hosts' narration	A different dynamic than interviews, though still usually led by the host(s)	Actors or the host reading materials such as books, letters, diaries	Recordings of sonic phenomena, sound-scapes, or archival materials, etc.	Songs or instrumental pieces that either directly relate or pass comment upon the topic
0-					
Etc.					

Develop (your series)

I generally would not call one-off standalone episodes podcasts. You may wish to record audio and put it online (e.g. if you are a teacher for your students), or you may contribute your expertise to the making of audio documentaries for radio (the BBC does this and has made excellent podcast series in collaboration with scholars). But the uploading of an audio lecture or another piece of audio is not a podcast. Podcasts exist as part of series. These series can be subscribed to, and, crucially, relationships are formed between the listener and the host over time (even if the host does not invite direct listener interaction).

This means that you need to think not only about what goes into a podcast episode, but how those episodes relate to each other. Do all episodes need to be listened to in order? Are they standalone? Are there mini-series within the overall series? Are there seasons?

If you are making a series where one story, idea, or argument unfolds over many episodes, thinking carefully about the relationship is especially important. An example is *How to Build a Stock Exchange: Making Finance Fit for the Future* by Philip Roscoe, in which he tells us how we might build a (better) stock exchange over an entire series by exploring different aspects of finance. The *Disasters Deconstructed Podcast* by Ksenia Chmutina and Jason von Meding has episodes that can be listened to in isolation but, after having a more scattered approach in their first series, settled on a theme for their second series so that listeners would come back to explore the topic and not just listen to standalone episodes.

Even if you are making a series of episodes that can be listened to in isolation, you will probably want to employ devices that forge connections between the episodes and create familiarity and intimacy through repetition (see Exercise 4).

If, in your role as a teacher, you have given your students the chance to make a podcast as an assignment then you may wish to provide a common intro and outro to put the series in context. If you have created a lecture series, then you may wish to have recurrent sections that re-cap previous lectures or where you ask the students to contemplate certain questions, which could then be combined with a short musical break.

It's probably the case that you'll develop your series in an ongoing fashion once you start publishing and work out what works and what doesn't, but that doesn't mean thinking about it before you start is a bad idea.

How have scholars developed their series?

> 00:03:55,000 With *Hardcore History* I sat down, and we had an entire blank chalkboard with anything available you wanted to do. And having no parameters at all was enthralling, but you don't even kind of know where to begin. I mean, you put a mark on the chalkboard and say, 'OK, do we start?' I mean, you don't even know. The parameters aren't even clear. So that was part of the fun and part of the 'What do we do now?' And I think if you listen, as a matter of fact, I know if you listen to a bunch of our early shows, you can watch the evolution. Any sort of content, a television series or anything, you can watch the same thing happen where you watch the first shows, and it almost seems like the characters haven't quite found their footing yet. It took 10 or 12 episodes of *Seinfeld* before *Seinfeld* was *Seinfeld*. And I find that's the same with most shows because you're also seeing what works. You're getting listener feedback, you're dropping stuff that didn't turn out the way you expected and adding stuff that worked better than intended. There's a lot of that going on so that at a certain point you begin to solidify into something that resembles your original plan in some ways, but maybe doesn't resemble it at all in other ways. And it's a crafting of what you thought initially and what you learnt along the way. And that describes the *Hardcore History* development pretty well.
>
> **Dan Carlin, Hardcore History**

> 00:20:36,000 I think part of it is just realising that people are going to want to stick around and listen more if you give them a compelling story, because otherwise you become a podcast where, you know, you have an episode about each of these topics and people might listen if they need to know about this topic and that's kind of

what Season One was a little bit like. And I know a lot of educators who use Season One to give to their students to learn about different topics. But we want to build an audience base that actually comes back for weekly content and compelling stories about disasters. I think it's something that we need to stick with for the future rather than just doing topics which might attract somebody to listen once off because they're interested in a topic.

Jason von Meding, Disasters Deconstructed Podcast

00:38:09,000 There's a lot of goofy little things that I gradually added to the show over time. I do try to think as consciously as I can about what the format is and why I'm choosing the format I'm choosing. You listen to a lot of podcasts? Right. You probably heard a lot of people who include sponsored content and whatnot where they give you this bullshit speel, 'do sleep on a mattress? Well, here's a mattress you'll really like. It's a great mattress. And order the mattress and use our code and you'll get it' just like fucking hell, you know? I mean, it's so corny and lame and cheesy. I'm like, you have a job, do you really need to do sponsored content? I mean, why are you doing this? So at a certain point, about a year ago, I got so fed up with all the damn sponsored content that I decided to put commercials into all of my programmes. Like I said, I collect records. I have a bunch of commercials and stuff that I've collected on 45s or LPs from like from the '60s and '70s. I just started sticking in commercials for things that no longer exist [laughs] as bullshit, fake sponsored content, just as a way of like trolling the idea of having sponsored content in a podcast. And so that was fun for a while. I kind of got bored with that a little bit. Now I try to think of something that would be funny in relation to whatever the content of the podcast is, like a thematic song or recording or something else that kind of reminds me in some way of what somebody is talking about in a somewhat oblique fashion, but as a commentary on how might we think about the subject matter of this particular conversation.

Brian L. Frye, Ipse Dixit

Exercise 4 Thinking across Episodes

Do all episodes need to be listened to in order? Are they standalone? Are there mini-series within the over-all series? Please fill in the 'podcasting across episodes' table.

Episode Number	Contained 'story' What is the actual episode about? This is usually what will take up most of the podcast's content	Series development Usually **either** a serial **or** a thematically linked series		Scaffolding content elements or devices that can be used to link the episodes together			
		Serial structure narrative What comes when (and why) as you work through the bigger picture	Thematic structure link to the overall time What links this episode to the theme? The link might be the content, but also the form (e.g. interviews with X)	Recurring elements jingle at the start/end, 'traditional' question, piece of sound, 'x of the week', etc.	Recaps whole segments dedicated to an overview, listeners' letters about the last episode	'Previously on…' usually for serials, appears towards the beginning of the episode	'Next time on…' usually only for serials, appears at the end of the episode
1							
2							
3							
4							
5 Etc.							

Note: This exercise was developed collaboratively with Dumitrita Holdis.

Write (for the ear)

When writing anything, actually before writing anything, you should have your audience in mind. I know my audience for this book is not experienced podcast producers or audio technicians. In fact, I hope they will never read this book as they'll get very angry at the way in which I simplify the discussions on microphones below. Whom you imagine your audience to be will determine how you write, and because there is no such thing as 'the general public', it's good to have a specific person or group in mind. It's totally fine to be narrow and specialised; if you're writing for a specialised audience, you will be able to use specialised terms. Furthermore, if your niche is scholars who work on the same topic as you, then it'll change the way you introduce and explain topics, and if your audience does not share your expertise then you will have to spend more time giving background information. Writing for a different audience will probably also change your tone of writing and speaking. Is your audience the 30 people in the world working on your topic? Your class of students? People who wished they'd studied philosophy at university but were persuaded to do accounting by their parents and are now miserable (and rich)?

Keeping your audience in mind, you need to decide on how much detail you will write. Some people are fine with a rough plan of what they are planning to say, others use bullet points, whilst some develop full scripts. *A History of Philosophy Without Any Gaps* by Peter Adamson is an example of a great podcast which, for some episodes, has a detailed script of pretty much everything that will be said. *Hardcore History* with Dan Carlin is an example of a great podcast in which there is a plan of what will be covered and how, but no detailed script. Peter Adamson is a philosophy professor who turned his scripts into a book series. Dan Carlin is a history enthusiast who used to work in talk radio. They both have different talents and trainings that they employ to make very successful history podcasts in very different ways. You will know what type of person you are from your experiences speaking in public at conferences, classrooms, or court. When I make podcast episodes, I use a mix of detail: some parts are scripted, some parts have bullet points, and some parts are quite free and open.

Writing a script is not only about scripting single-voiced narrations. It's also about thinking through how you and a co-host might structure a conversation or how one of you might read a script and other hosts respond. I would say the biggest danger in multiple-host scholarly podcasting is forgetting who the audience is and, even worse, that the audience is there.

Whichever way you write, clarity is vital. You may wish to deliberately confuse the listener – i.e. take them to one place to reveal something else – but this is different from being confusing through poor writing. There are many confusingly written academic texts. However, when I get lost reading something, I can skip back a couple of pages to check my understanding and re-read key passages. Whilst it is possible to skip back a few seconds on a podcast, for the most part, it is far less easy to do so, and listeners are much more likely to switch off than relisten to a segment. Podcasting is much more linear than writing!

If you feel yourself getting lost in your own writing, ask yourself, 'what am I saying?' 'who is doing what to whom?' 'what is happening?' 'how does what is happening relate to the last thing I said?' You may wish to flag up structure more acutely than you would in your writing for the eye. Letting the listener know where they have been and what they might expect helps them not to get lost along the way. For example:

> 'We've just had a great discussion with French sociologist Pierre Bourdieu about why he writes so densely and next up I'm going to delve into the academic industry that has sprung up in the English-speaking academe in the last decades: interpreting difficult to understand dead continental theorists'.

If you do want to mention academic works, as you often might, then the name of the author and the text are enough. You don't need to include the full reference, you can use the show notes to do that (which people can find on their podcast apps or a website, if you have one).

If you are writing a full script – or even if you want to think about how you are speaking – then you might want to tone down the wordiness. Academics love to create long complex sentences. For example, instead of writing, 'Academics love to create long complex sentences', if I were a 'proper scholar' I would've written, 'there is a tendency amongst a considerable number of those who work in and around academia, to produce complexified and lengthy sentences in the works they produce, whether it be in a journal article or book format'. The longer and more complex sentence says more and has more nuance, and you may want to argue that it is a good one for academic writing because of this, but I am not convinced at all that it sounds better when spoken in a podcast form.

If you want to reduce the academic tendency for wordiness then my number one piece of advice would be to be 'lively'.

The passive voice might work well in writing, but it leaves listeners cold when used in podcasting. For instance, hear the difference between '*a decision was made* to award Ian M. Cook the Academic Podcasting Book of the Year award by scholars this month' versus 'This month, scholars *decided* to award Ian M. Cook "Academic Podcasting Book of the Year"'. The second one sounds much livelier and works way better when spoken.

This liveliness can be furthered if you limit your use of nominalisations (i.e. phrases in which nouns are formed by verbs, where often the nouns end in -tion or -ness). The use of these weakens the action you are describing. For instance: 'Ian's book is *in need of some reorganisation*' versus 'Ian *needs to reorganise his book*'. In short, when expressing action, use verbs more often than nouns.

Vary your sentence length. Really. It's going to make your writing sound livelier. If all of your sentences are the same length, it makes it harder to concentrate on what you say. In general, you are going to want to aim for shorter sentences than you might use in your academic writing: if you need to take a big breath in the middle of your sentence then it's probably too long. You are also going to want to avoid em-dashes – those breaks in the middle of the sentences which academics like to use to clarify to explain something – when writing your script. Sometimes they are needed in written text, but people cannot hear such forms of punctuation (just like they can't hear brackets).

Take a look at your script and ask yourself if all of the words are really needed in the sentence, especially those words that we like to use before we get to the point of what we are trying to say. Due to the fact… this may serve of as example of how… in the event of you reading it… it will show that… one of the most important… and so on. Of course, sometimes they really are needed. But ask yourself if they are really needed when you speak, if they are really needed every time you express an idea, and if they are killing the liveliness in your writing.

Try to be a bit less vague. Or, to be more precise, nouns can sometimes be more useful than pronouns in your sentences. Compare, 'there are suggestions that Ian's book is lacking in research' versus 'Ian's book lacks research'.

Do you use contractions when you talk? If so, you should also probably use them when you write scripts that you're going to say out loud. 'I would've if I could've, but I couldn't so I didn't' is no excuse. You can. There's no such phrase as 'cannot' in podcasting, just 'can't'.

Finally, and maybe most importantly, sound is your friend. But like all friendships, you need to work on it. You may be a very dynamic speaker, but you might not be, and so it could help to underline words you want to add emphasis on. Likewise, you may be fully aware of when to leave a dramatic pause but, if not, then writing [dramatic pause] into your scripts can help immensely. I have listened to many an academic podcast that run on and on without pause, and it becomes impossible to follow. It's not a race to finish your podcast as quickly as possible. Further to this, sound, including music, can be layered under voices completely changing the feeling of the words that are being spoken. And if there is sound running underneath when someone speaks, then suddenly stopping the music can focus the listener's attention upon the words. Of course, good use of sound takes practice, so don't worry if it sounds cheesy or awkward at first. Test what combinations of sounds and music work well with your own or other voices.

What about others? How have they thought about their writing?

> 00:13:37,000 You know what happened to me? I really didn't like to write. Somehow, I was always very intimidated by writing because I felt like that's a different level, that's when you go to school and you have to prove yourself as a kid with all of this added anxiety and with this need for validation and you had to be proper. It just felt like there's so many rules around writing. And I actually didn't have so many problems speaking, I think I can speak fairly well.
>
> All of these rules and anxieties, all of the fears and the expectations that came with writing, at some point they disappeared because I realised that I'm not saying what I'm writing when I'm writing for a podcast, I'm just writing what I'm saying. I reversed this relationship between writing and speaking at some point and it became quite easy because I realised, I don't have to write something that then I will speak for the podcast. Rather, it's the other way around. I'm taking all of these words and I'm writing them down so I remember them better. I somehow flipped the relationship between writing and speech, and I think that really unblocked my writer's block.
>
> **Dumitriţa Holdiş, Down, but Not Out**

00:16:04,000 Because I've been an academic, my writing is so dry I don't like it. It's not fun and I don't know how to be fun without sounding just embarrassing. But in podcasting, it's totally fine. I'm more freewheeling and it's just easier.

Carrie Gillon, The Vocal Fries

00:19:52,000 I think emotional intelligence is a big component to being a good scientific communicator, because we have to understand that what we are saying is not for ourselves. And a lot of the times that takes practice to realise that in everything I'm saying, I have to have empathy and understand how you are going to interpret that. That is the key to good scientific communication.

Stephanie Caligiuri, The People's Scientist

00:03:21,000 I listened to crime thrillers and loads of different things just to get ideas. I was I'm like, 'well, there's this whole world out there, amazing stuff going on'. And then I thought, 'how am I going to approach this?' Because it could be as dry as hell. And, you know, I am constrained in these podcasts because they're driven by the [Sociology A Level] curriculum, which I think itself is problematic. But anyway, it's quite limited in its view, but I thought, 'Right. So, I'm going to give birth to two characters. They are going to be my new babies. They need to tell my story because it's much more interesting if there's two people'. I gave birth to two characters, and I thought of their personalities and their relationship and then I decided she was gonna be more clever than him, and then just made sure that their relationship was different to a teacher-student relationship in formality, but actually that's kind of what was going on.

Laura Pountney, Audiopi Sociology

00:29:55,000 Audio footnotes is something we developed, which is the idea that, 'how do you believe the host of the show if he's just told you he's not a historian?' So I try to back up stuff with little, teeny quotes from people who you should probably trust at least more than the host. And then what ended up happening? Because, as you well know, experts can differ on stuff... and so we started including sometimes contrasting views. 'If you're not an expert and I'm not, well, how can you choose between the experts?' So, we would have audio footnotes that contrasted each other. And people loved that because that's introducing things like historiography to regular non-historians.

Dan Carlin, Hardcore History

Exercise 5 Scripting an Opening

Write the opening to a podcast you would like to make. Your intro might be fully scripted, bullet pointed, or just a rough plan. You might wish to consider setting the topic, saying why it's important, introducing a character (e.g. if you plan to interview someone), or describing a location.

Speak (with your voice to your audience)

There is no such thing as a 'good podcasting voice'. What we have come to appreciate as a 'good voice' is culturally constructed, inscribed with problematic class, regional, native-speaker, and gendered norms. One of the wonderful things about podcasting is that it has increased the diversity of voices that we hear. Do not be shy about being different, weird, quiet, loud, fast or slow, or whatever. It's your voice and we don't all have to sound like bad imitations of breakfast radio broadcasters. What do scholars who podcast sound like? They sound like you.

But this doesn't mean that you cannot develop your podcasting voice. To develop it, you need to find it, and to find it you need to listen to it, learn it, and use it. You don't 'have' a voice, it's not a static thing you have no control over. Rather, you 'use' a voice. It can do a lot. We'll get to recording techniques soon, but before reading on, try recording your voice on your phone or computer and listen back to it carefully. Read something out and record it. Then speak freestyle and record it. Now take a moment to listen to it.

Whether you're speaking freestyle or with bullet points you are going to start to notice certain things that you do, and certain things that you don't do but might want to consider doing in the future. A good place to start is by paying attention to the tone; listen to inflection, to peaks and troughs, to your speed, onto which words you are putting emphasis. Depending on the podcast you are making, you might want to try using your voice in different ways. In general, you are probably not going to want to have too much punch like a cheesy talk show host, nor sound too flat as if you were a stilted academic reading a paper at a conference; you probably also don't want to sound like a sickly earnest politician (e.g. Tony Blair) or, if you're a teacher, slip too much into your teaching voice.

We all have moments when we zone out when listening to someone speak, be it on a podcast or elsewhere. Some of this can be solved by not staying too long on a certain topic or type of content delivery (people can concentrate for around 15–20 minutes), but there are also ways in which you can work on how you speak to keep people engaged. As with writing, varying sentence length can be useful and, if you're speaking for quite some time, summing up what you've just said at the end can help reinforce what you wish to say.

Once you start to listen back to your voice in longer recordings or when you listen to podcasters who don't always speak in as engaged a way as you might like, you begin to notice that certain people, possibly even including yourself, struggle with energy drop-offs or with eating their words rather than saying them. You can train your voice to overcome both of these issues. Low energy relates to poor breath support. You can practise doing different types of breathing from big open breathing to short shallow breaths regularly to improve this. Another tip is to hold your finger out in front of you at a distance so that when you blow you can just feel your breath. Blow on it ten times every day and, after some time, you should hopefully be able to keep your energy high to the end of long sentences. You can also train yourself not to eat your words or mumble by working on your enunciation. Look into the mirror and practise saying words slowly to yourself. Tongue twisters are great for this, for example, 'Peter Piper picked a peck of pickled podcasters, a pack of peppered podcasters Peter Piper picked, if Peter Piper picked a pack of pickled podcasters, where's the peppered podcasters Peter Piper picked?'

Training your voice is one element, but you can also do things on the day to help your voice. Make sure you're hydrated and choose warm drinks, neither too cold nor too hot, as this will be good for your vocal cords. When you sit to speak, relax your posture, don't slouch over the microphone, but also don't sit up tense like a scolded schoolchild. Slouching puts pressure on your ribcage making it hard to breathe in. Before you start, breathe into your nose for three seconds and then exhale out your mouth for nine. Now work on your lips. Do some humming, some ahhhing and some buzzing. Put your tongue up on the top of your mouth, say 'la' a lot, say 'r' a lot. Pretend you're Freddy Mercury at Wembley. Once the recording has started, remember to breathe.

Energy can be played with; you can choose which of your words have more or less drive, which are quieter and louder, which you choose to slow down for and speed up for. It's not an A-to-B exercise in which you need to put all your words into the microphone. Play with your words.

Facial expressions change your delivery. Try speaking when smiling and when not smiling. Listen to the difference. Which suits your style better? Play some more: try speaking in different accents.

Even if you are reading a script, try to sound like you're not; imagine you're telling a story to a person you like and trust rather than reading out a script to a big audience. One of the biggest tells that people are reading is when their energy level drops off at the end of a sentence. Some people also do this when they are speaking without a script, just sort of let their idea trail off at the end and finish with a mumble. You can practise expressing yourself strongly throughout your idea, focusing on a consistent volume. If you are reading, then looking up at the end of the sentence can reduce drop off. Breathe normally when talking. Relax.

Finally, your microphone is an instrument; learn it. We'll discuss how to record in the next section, but similar to how you can learn how to use your voice by listening to it, you can do the same with whatever microphone you're using. Try speaking closer to it, further away, from the side, straight down the middle. Try speaking through it. Feel how bad it sounds when you shout into it or when you're scared to get too close. Do you hear plosive p's and hissing s's?

What advice do podcasters have about finding and using their voices?

> 00:49:24,000 It also has something to do with voice and finally finding what your voice can be. Our colleague at the radio, she has a really, really beautiful radio voice. And we had this trouble, 'oh our voices are so terrible', 'our tone, our voice, how you hear it, it's terrible. We have to train it'. I think I have a podcast voice that I use for podcasting. It's not only that the tone of the voice changes, but also how you are able to articulate sentences and put words together. And, well, that appears to be important in academia.
>
> **Maria Martelli, contrasens**

00:07:56,000 The thing that I always did best in the talk radio format, that I was in at the time, was at the beginning of the show where you would lay out a monologue or something that you wanted to setup as the conversational piece of the day. And I was always sort of inspired energy-wise. And I talk a lot more slowly than I used to. And I was always a bit loud and it was always the part that I enjoyed the most.

But it was almost a little like a superpower and I was worried about losing it. And so, I remember we would do the early podcasts and we would do them just the same way I would do a radio show, a live take all the way through. And I remember I coughed once and I stopped and I said, 'oh, my God'. And we were 20 minutes into it or something like that. I said, 'we've got to start over'. And the person looked at me and said, 'we have to start over?' I said, 'Yeah. I said, we got to'. And he goes, 'Why wouldn't you just edit that?' And I said, 'Oh, I'm not getting into editing. If we start getting into editing, I'm going to lose my chops. I'm not going to be able to do this anymore. I'll never be able to go back to radio'.

Well, long story short, we got far from there pretty quickly. And now the shows I do are so long, you could never go in there and just record them all in one. But it took a while for me to say that maybe I'm not going to worry anymore about losing my chops for a business I didn't want to go back into any way. But back in 2005 nobody even knew what podcasts were. And so, trying to say, 'no, no, no, I'm throwing all my lot in with these podcast things' was a difficult thing to do back then. Less difficult to do now.

Dan Carlin, Hardcore History

00:24:44,000 And it really was helpful for me to think about how some of the tonalities that are associated with young women's conversation are often disparaged and treated as less trustworthy, less smart, those kinds of things. And it reminded me of how important I think it is to reflect that there are great brains inside of all kinds of heads that have all kinds of voices coming out of them. And, you know, I am probably more flexible in the way I speak, depending on who I'm speaking to. And I think that really is a function of being in a very hierarchical space. I'm not going to talk to my much older, much senior colleagues in the same way as I might talk to my hairdresser. You know, it is more a matter of making everyone around me feel comfortable and make myself feel comfortable in that space. And that's a kind of code switching I think most of us do every day.

Maria Sachiko Cecire, In Theory

00:34:43,000 I have these students with, I think, beautiful, wonderful, fun, quirky voices that are like, 'I hate my voice'. I'm like, 'no, you know, why don't you go with that and play it up'. You can take the most interesting part of yourself and try to do something with it.

Mark Pedelty, Public Lands Podcast

00:36:38,000 I guess if you're not familiar with podcasts and you listen for the first time and then you hear someone always stumbling over his words and rephrasing their sentences all the time, it might be annoying for some people. But I think that that is what podcasts are about; it's a process, you really listen to someone develop their ideas as they speak. And that's sometimes really interesting.

Johanna Sebauer, BredowCast

00:16:45,000 My students invariably have an accent because they're not native English speakers. But I'm not trying to get them to change their voices or change the nuances in their delivery to be more English or to be anything. I'm like, 'no, I'm looking for your authentic voice'. So that's also key in using vocabulary that you wouldn't use casually. And don't start inserting words that you're not familiar with, like use your natural conversational tone and words that you're familiar with to tell your story. I think we have to pull off the same thing in the classroom.

How do we work on improving it? I'll tell you how you work on improving. It's really simple. And I can tell you this from high school, when one of my high school teachers told me, you practise reading the newspaper or practise reading articles. The thing is, though, that newspaper articles aren't written for radio, but you have to go through and you mark and you read it in a way that people can understand. And there's no costs for that. You don't have to pay a voice coach or anything, but you just sit down with an article, and you just read it out loud.

Kim Fox, podcast teacher and scholar

00:41:32,000 We speak before we do every recording about how we're gonna be projecting our voices. We're teachers, so we know. The best advice we give to guests before they start is get a fist, put it in front of a microphone, that's how far away you need to be. Don't talk at us. Talk into the microphone and talk through it. But most importantly, smile when you're speaking. You can literally hear a smile when someone's talking and that makes you want to listen. You can hate someone who's smart, but you can't hate someone who's smiling. We were fortunate enough to have had some excellent teacher training and we've had voice coaches come into our schools and universities and teach us how we can project our voice to convey certain messages. On the way to recordings, I often find myself practising my 'Hello and welcome!'.

Jack Symes, The Panpsycast

00:51:43,000 Not everybody is that interesting to listen to just in terms of their tone. I mean, you go to academic conferences and the amount of times I've just lost the will to live when somebody has just got their head down reading a paper that they could have just handed me. I think podcasting kind of represents that crossover moment when somebody actually realises, 'well, I'm giving a presentation, I'm presenting myself as well as the information'. And that's why I think that academic podcasting is perhaps not in the place that it could be, because the idea of just taping a lecture is not a podcast to me. You know, everybody could tape all their lectures and put them online. And it doesn't give you that sense of the creativity of podcasting. So that has to be factored in and that takes time and effort. And it's a skill that has to be learnt. If you want to do it well.

Dario Llinares, The Cinematologists and podcast scholar

Exercise 6   Writing and Speaking

Record the introduction to a podcast you would like to make that you wrote for Exercise 5. Don't worry now about recording quality; a smartphone or other simple mic is fine. Now listen back to your recording along with your script and pay attention to both its listenability (i.e. how well it is written for the ear and not the eye) and how your voice sounds (i.e. how well you have used your voice).

   Now re-write your script. Include annotations as to where you might want to pause, ideas you might want to emphasise, and so on. Re-record, listen back.

Interview (for tape)

Interviews are by far the most common format in scholarly podcasting. A lot of academic podcasts consist of scholars interviewing other scholars. Some are absolutely wonderful, and some are less so. Some of the bad ones often suffer from poor choice of guest, underdeveloped interview technique, incomprehensible questions that seem to be designed to show off the interviewer's intelligence rather than grow a conversation, a meandering structure, under-researched questions, and questions that start but don't seem to really have an end. Interviewing is a craft and, like other crafts, it's something that can be nurtured and developed over time.

Those of us who work in the social sciences and humanities are used to making interviews as one of our core methods. However, an interview for 'tape' is different than interviewing within an ethnographic or oral history project, for example. There is a difference between interviewing somebody, or a group of people, for the purpose of research and for the purpose of a podcast (though there are occasions when it can be both). There are different ethical considerations when a public can hear the voice of those we research amongst, changes in how a conversation might be guided when we keep a listener's interests rather than a researcher's in mind, time constraints if we want to keep a conversation manageable when it comes to editing and assembling the podcast, and different considerations in a choice of guest.

Before interviewing or leading a group discussion with any one person or group, the first question should be 'what is my objective?': is it part of a podcast/story or is it the whole podcast/story. For example, if I am making a podcast about scholarly podcasts, I could interview 101 scholars who make podcasts and take excerpts from those podcasts and weave them together to form a larger narrative. Or I could make 101 podcasts on the topic, with each podcast a different interview. A change in objective would change the way I guide the conversation, both in terms of overall structure (e.g. do I need the structure to work as a standalone podcast conversation or not?) and in terms of the responses I get from people (e.g. do I need people's answers to be self-contained or can it be a back-and-forth discussion?).

Once the objective is settled, you can then do some more detailed preparation. It is a given that you need to research the topic, but you should also – if possible – research the guest. If you can find recordings of your potential inter-viewee online then listen to how they speak, how they respond to questions, if there are familiar tales they like to tell, and so on. You also need to prepare your guest or guests for the interview or group discussion. Make sure they understand the purpose, that it will be public, that the conversation will be edited down, and any rules you might want to have in place for the discussion (such as order of speaking, giving others space, and so on).

Sometimes the guests request for questions to be sent in advance, and sometimes you might think it's a good idea. Sean Guillory from *SRB Podcast* sends the questions a day in advance to reduce his academic guests' nervousness. Usually I do not send questions but rather the topics I wish to discuss and in what order a couple of days before the interview or discussion. This allows the guest(s) to prepare a little bit, but not too much. It can also lead to a better-structured discussion, as the guests don't say everything you wish to talk about in the first five minutes. However, if the interview seems like it's going badly because the guest has over-prepared, then I start asking different questions.

You also must craft your questions. It's good to ask yourself, 'what do I want to know?' and 'why do I want to know it?' This will then help you work out how to phrase questions. If I am going to interview someone or lead a group discussion for what will end up a 20–30-minute seg-ment, I usually only have three big questions. I have sub-questions under each big theme to follow up, but if I want to get in depth into a topic then having more than three themes means I'll never get to the later ones; these three questions or themes give me the overall shape of the interview. It's then a good idea to try and anticipate what your guest or guests might say. Of course, you hope they will say something that surprises you, but by thinking ahead you can also start to think of what your possible follow-up questions might be.

The reason I do all this prep is not so that I have a mechanical unsurprising interview but rather so that I can concentrate on listening to the guest and thus feel comfortable going off-script and exploring the surprising. Listening is one of the hardest things to do, but the best interviewers are great listeners; they listen intensely so that their follow-up questions can take the conversation to revealing places. It's hard to listen if you are worried about not knowing what the next question might be in case you can't think of a good follow-up. Prep gives you a safety net so you can follow your fascination.

It's important to ask questions with the audience in mind. What are they interested in? What do they already know? What might they want to know further? What do they not know that they don't know they want to know but you, having done lots of research, think they want to know? There are different types of questions – open-ended questions, closed questions, exploratory questions, deliberately naive questions, leading questions, questions that challenge your guest(s) opinions/research, questions that give them space to explain... the types of question you choose will depend on the guest(s) and the topic and purpose of the podcast; however, there are some general pointers that apply in most situations. Do not ask more than one question at once, as for the most part people will reply only to the last question. If someone doesn't answer the question, or barely answers the question, rephrase it, and repeat it. If a guest is giving banal answers, try putting words into their mouth that you think they wouldn't say to elicit a response (e.g. Interviewer: Ian, I think you only wrote a book about scholarly podcasting to get rich, right? Ian: Woah, let me tell you about my royalties …). Remember, it's not only what people say that's important but also how they say it: the emotion in their voice, the way they pause, if they are being ironic. Allow for moments of silence, often it means people are thinking – and thinking is a good thing. People also tend to fill up silence with words eventually. Make eye contact; don't stare down at your questions. And listen, listen, listen.

You are not only recording words to be written down but sounds to be heard. This means not only paying attention to the sound of someone's voice, as mentioned above, but also the environment. We will move on to recording shortly, but in an interview situation you are more than likely going to want to have the voice heard as clearly as possible. This means thinking about noises from mobile phones, fans, fridges, air conditioning units, traffic, and so on. Try to anticipate your recording conditions. If you can, suggest somewhere quiet to meet but also somewhere with decent acoustics; in general, smaller places with soft furnishings to absorb sounds are best. It is also important to think of sound when you arrive at the interview location (e.g. you might want to turn off TVs and fans).

You also need to politely boss your guests around. Usually this means telling them where to sit, asking them to turn off their phone(s) and, if you're sitting down, not to bang the table or fidget with items. These are the most common, but it could be anything that makes unwanted noise. For instance, I've had to ask someone to take off a necklace made of shells. Finally, it may seem as if none of this matters when you're conducting interviews online, but it does. I always tell guests to be in a quiet place, to put their phone on 'flight mode', and to use headphones (so I don't hear myself through their computer mic).

There are a lot of different interview styles and techniques, and many podcasters will give contrasting suggestions about how to prepare and conduct an interview.

What are some of the suggestions on how to interview well for a podcast?

00:07:51,000 If a podcast is done well, the people in the podcast are meant to be sort of the avatar for the listener, in a sense, like the advocate for the listener, in that they should be asking all of the same questions that a listener who's experiencing this information for the first time would probably have, 'What does this person need to know next?' 'What context needs to be given here?' Maybe it happens naturally or else it's really well planned out by the producer of the podcast, but it should end up feeling like you did participate in a conversation, even though you weren't literally participating in it.

Lori Beckstead, podcast scholar

00:03:49,000 It's tempting to not want to look like a fool when you're talking, especially as your audience grows, but you're going to look like a fool in the sense that you can't match the knowledge of the person that you're interviewing and that shouldn't be your goal.

Bonni Stachowiak, Teaching in Higher Ed

00:13:36,000 Rather than being the person talking, be the person listening, because I think as law professors, we are used to talking. And over time, we get less and less good at listening. And so, I try to do more listening and less talking.

Brian L. Fyre, Ipse Dixit

00:40:12,000 You may also know about this, Ian, but one of my favourite things to do in an interview is just shut up and let people keep talking, kind of back off, leave a little more blank space for people to say things. And it doesn't always work for the podcast medium, because people get so, so concerned that there is silence that they want to keep saying something. And that's often when you get the best responses to your interview that you'll then put in an article, but that's not what the podcast medium is. But I think my interview style is more kind of backing off and having people maybe fill in a little more.

Evelyn Lamb, My Favorite Theorem

00:40:18,000 Some of the first podcasts we did were really focused questions, but then by the end of it we started being more comfortable with improvising and with asking better questions.

Maria Martelli, contrasens

00:43:30,000 I don't know that there's an interview style that I particularly like or dislike. I think it's probably less about my style because I'm the consistent factor in it, but I wanted it to be less about my style than about the individuals, and capturing the individuals, rather than fitting them in. I talk a lot about [long running BBC Radio interview show] *Desert Island Discs* because I've listened to loads of them now and with shoehorning every person into the same format, even though you capture their own stories, it became a bit regimented over time. I was actually getting quite bored of the number of songs being the same, the number of minutes of each song, and it was kind of forced. The conversation seems clipped off at certain points just to fit the format. And I didn't really want to do that.

Heather May Morgan, Higher Education, Human Employment

00:57:12,000 I do a lot of qualitative interviews. I did so for my research before, and I have the tendency to let people speak. At length. We all do. If we do qualitative interviews, that's what we do. But if you want a podcast to be concise, clear and fit within 15 minutes, you have to interview differently. And that's something I still have to learn. It's something I noticed after the first few interviews I did. One interview, one of the very first ones, where I wasn't so clear about what I wanted, but was with a very senior person, and it ended up being, I think, an hour or an hour and fifteen minutes. I didn't know how to be friendly, polite, and yet, you know, stop. This is really something to be learnt. You have to, I suppose, switch your academic hat with, not entirely, but to some extent, that of a journalist hat. You need to just be a different interviewer. That's what I think.

Fiona Seiger, The Migration Podcast

00:25:27,000 But I guess maybe somewhat arrogantly, I would say that I think the comparative advantage of academics podcasting is that we just know more about the area. You're able to draw on your own knowledge, your own experience, to ask slightly different questions or to draw parallels with things that you know from your own work. I think overall that produces a different type of interview in reach, depth, and knowledge. It's certainly, in my case, probably more wooden than what a professional broadcaster would do, but it just produces a different type of interview. And I guess experience shows there's an audience for that.

Dave McRae, Talking Indonesia

00:18:05,000 There are other really great astronomy podcasts out there, but it does make a difference being the professionals. I still work as an actual astronomy researcher at the university. I'm really in-depth with the research. [Co-host] Dan [Cunnama] is also a professional astronomer. He's engaged with the science communication aspect with the observatory. And that makes a difference because we can ask the questions. We already, sort of, know the answers to the questions and so we can ask the relevant questions. And we also have a lot of science communication experience. We also understand what it is that the public probably doesn't understand. We can be the translators between the scientist and the public. And I think that's really the key here. We understand the jargon, we know how to ask a question following up on a sentence that's full of jargon. We know which are the essential aspects to define, which ones that we can define in the pre-interview. Essentially, we already understand the larger context of the story and so we don't need to spend so much time trying to figure that out. We already know and we can guide the questions around it.

Jacinta Delhaize, The Cosmic Savannah

00:50:29,000 I think academics as a whole are so immersed in their own world and their own interests, they don't stop to think about whether or not the audience is falling asleep... I think we have to stop and think outside ourselves for a bit and go, 'OK. This isn't about me. This is about whether or not you're interested, because if you're not interested this isn't working, and I need to think about how to fix it'.

Ann Wand, Coffee & Cocktails

00:38:45,000 Oh, it's really easy to make a bad podcast. Being self-absorbed, assuming that everyone loves whatever the topics are as much as you do, assuming that people understand them in the same depth as you do or get it the same way that you do. Alienating them so that it's almost like a little chuckle fest between you and a guest, loads of in-jokes that exclude the audience. Those are the ingredients of a really bad podcast. Loads of intrusive sound effects, poor attention to the quality of the audio. These sorts of things. So we try and address all that in our programmes.

We make sure that we put the audience front and centre. I always say to people when they join the *Naked Scientist*, 'who is the most important person in this room?' and they'll say, 'Oh, we know who you guys are, the team' and I say 'no, the audience are the most important people in the *Naked Scientist*, because if you have no audience, what's the point of turning up to work?' We're always thinking about the people who are listening and thinking, 'what do they want to know? Why do they want to know this? Why should they give up an hour of their life to listen to us?' It's a huge privilege for us to have their ears. Let's not waste it.

Chris Smith, The Naked Scientist

00:39:01,000 I come from a very working-class background. It was always sort of a struggle for me with my family, they didn't understand what I do and all those issues. To paraphrase Kurt Vonnegut, who said this about literature, it shouldn't disappear up its own arsehole, so to speak. There's a real danger in having a couple or more academics talking about something, if they're not very good at communicating more broadly, that the podcasts could disappear up its own arsehole. [Co-host] Evelyn [Lamb] is a professional mathematician, she just left academia [to work in journalism]. I think what's good about having the two of us is that we can keep the whole thing honest. I mean, we both have real mathematical chops, but we also are pretty good at communicating more broadly.

Kevin Knudson, My Favorite Theorem

00:51:09,000 There's an awful lot of people who will say, 'I want to do a podcast episode with you and talk to you about your work'. But then they don't learn anything about it beforehand. And I'm like, 'Your presence here is not helpful because you have no fucking idea what's going on. You have no idea what I'm talking about. You're asking me questions that are just making people dumber. Because your question is totally useless, you know?' I mean, it's hard to ask a dumb question that's actually helpful. You have to think about it and figure out what matters. You have to think about something long enough to understand the research in order to understand what somebody else needs to understand in order to make sense of it. And you can't do that if you don't do the work in advance. I didn't have a driver's licence for most of my adult life, so I spent many decades riding the bus everywhere because I like to listen to what people have to say, whatever I find interesting and amusing, slowly and carefully and quietly.

Brian L. Frye, Ipse Dixit

00:13:30,000 [Preparation] includes having a pre-conversation with the interviewee where we just sit down together for half an hour, an hour and discuss, 'OK, what is interesting about the subject that we want to talk about'. And after that, I'll prepare some sort of structure, maybe three main aspects that I want to touch on.

Johanna Sebauer, BredowCast

00:04:56,000 We wanted to really keep in-depth interviews, but I think this idea is also adapting all the time. So sometimes a person is central in our podcasts, but we also really would like to make documentaries where a topic is central, so you interview more people.

Anne van Mourik, NIOD Rewind Podcast on War & Violence

00:30:22,000 I send people questions literally the day before. I don't want them to overprepare, you know, they wrote books on this, they know this stuff already. They may have to, like, refresh their memory on some things. I don't feel like giving questions in advance is a problem, at least I haven't experienced a problem. If anything, academics can sometimes be skittish folk and kind of unsure of themselves. Graduate school, and academia and to some extent, is a constant assault on the ego where you're being constantly criticised. It's my way to give my guests some kind of comfort, some idea of what I am interested in, just to put them at ease.

Sean Guillory, SRB Podcast

00:47:20,000 Obviously there's some surprises, but in an interview you should be like a lawyer going into court. You're supposed to know everything that's gonna happen, as much as you can. You don't sit down and go, 'Who the hell are you? What do you do?'

Mariel Carr, Distillations

00:25:23,000 Usually, what I'll do is shape the narrative arc of the interview beforehand. I read the book and I shape it out and then I do a little preliminary chat with them when we sit down for like five minutes and I just get a feel for what the rhythm of their responses are. I ask them a question and sense, 'is this a person that's going to talk, talk, talk, or is this a person that I'm going to have to continue to pull stuff out of?' I doubt it just seems like small talk to them, but I'm measuring their type of response so I can say, 'did I prepared too many questions, too few, what's going on here?'

And then I'll spend five minutes just saying like, 'all right, let me give you an idea of what we're going to cover here.' And I'll just tell them, 'we're going to hit this point from your book. We're going to hit this point then this point, then this point. You don't have to get ahead of yourself'. And I put them at ease. I tell them 'I edit this. So, if you ever find yourself walking down a dead end and you want to stop and turn around, you can do that'. And through that little preliminary process, it puts most people at ease.

Blair Hodges, The Maxwell Institute Podcast

00:11:40,000 When I talk to researchers, I want to really get them in a mood where they don't speak to me, but they chat with me, you know, like they're not presenting their topic, but they are chatting with me. And that's sometimes not that easy because when they sit in front of a microphone, researchers tend to get stiff sometimes, because they're used to standing in front of a camera and being the expert on TV. And to then get them into the mood of chatting is sometimes not so easy, but it's a nice challenge. When I start I have super casual questions that I sometimes cut out and then when they drift off into something very abstract, I always try to pull them down to reality again and try to ask them like, 'OK, so how is this affecting my life or your life' or 'give me some concrete examples' or something like that.

Johanna Sebauer, BredowCast

00:46:43,000 Regardless of how much struggle there is, and there seems to be a lot, what's really good about it for me is that when I start recording, it's just this really flowing process that I am caught within. And it's just fascinating to listen to this person or ask them questions.

Maria Martelli, contrasens

00:18:59,000 For the real core interview stuff I'm just a great believer in the quiet space and the uninterrupted time, two hours of time or whatever. Once I have that, I sigh with relief because that's my spine. I'm always conscious of the little meta scenes as well that you will use to animate that, so it might be just in the same way that if you're doing a narrative written print journalism, a profile piece or something, you would observe the person a bit, but maybe like your ethnographic approach, you would just be like a fly on the wall with them in various normal activities that they do. I mean, the classic podcast trope is answering the phone or knocking, ringing on the bell, or getting into the car, starting the ignition. If I was working with an artist, I'd take them into their studio and they'd be setting up their stuff and they're getting their paints out or whatever. If I'm working on a journalism investigation, it might be, if it's a police person, it might be somebody rifling through files.

Siobhan McHugh, documentary podcaster
maker and podcast scholar

00:22:48,000 I have one really simple line of advice [to guests] before we start: if you have to choose a hard word or easy word, please choose the easy one.

Chris Smith, The Naked Scientist

Exercise 7 Creating Interview Questions

Based on the above considerations, develop a set of interview questions for a guest on your podcast. Think about the overarching structure, the sub-questions, possible ways to rephrase and probe ideas, and the overall length and purpose of the interview.

Record (words and other sounds)

You need four things if you want to record: sound (vibrations of air from voices and other things), a microphone (to transduce the vibrations), a recorder (to capture the transduced sound), and headphones (to allow you to hear what is being recorded).

Stop reading this and, if you're not in a library, clap your hands. What happens to that sound? It gets quieter as it moves further away and it travels through mediums like air, solid objects, and, if you're reading this in the bath, water. If you are reading this in space, then nobody can hear you clap. But if you are on earth then the vibrations can not only pass through solid objects but also bounce back. Imagine for a moment a recording studio. Even if you have never been in one, you know it has acoustic treatment on the walls: soft things and irregularly shaped things. This is so sound is absorbed and does not bounce around. Two properties of sound that you must be especially aware of are amplitude and frequency. Amplitude, or loudness, is a measure of how much energy is used to create a sound. When you edit sound, you can see this visually represented through height – i.e. the higher the crests of the soundwave, the louder the sound. Frequency is a measure of the speed of vibrations and is perceived as pitch. The lower the frequency the deeper the sound, the higher the frequencies the higher the sound. There is, of course, much more to be said about the physics of sound. However, I believe that just keeping in mind that sound moves, bounces, is absorbed, and can be louder/quieter and with higher/lower pitch is enough for us to get started with microphones.

Not all microphones are the same. They don't all have the same ability to capture pitch/frequency (their 'frequency response'), and not all microphones transduce sound the same way (i.e. 'dynamic' or 'condenser' mics). However, the most important consideration for the first-time podcaster is a microphone's differing polar patterns.

A microphone's polar pattern is a way of expressing its directional sensitivity to sound (or to be precise sound pressure). Or to put it more simply, a polar pattern shows us in which direction(s) a microphone picks up sound.

Different microphones are designed for different purposes and thus with different polar patterns. There are four basic polar patterns or shapes that you should be aware of (there are a lot more out there): cardioid – picks up sound from in front and sides of the mic in a heart shape; bi-directional (figure-8 shape) – picks up sound in front and behind; omni-directional – picks up sound from all around; shotgun (or hyper-cardioid) – picks up sound narrowly in front of the mic.

There are a lot of other names for different patterns. You can find out your mic's polar pattern with a quick search online or by looking at the manual. You will also see information about the drop-off rate, which refers to how well a mic picks up sound in relation to how far it is from the source.

The mic for any given situation depends on what you want to capture. But it will also depend on your ability to get hold of a mic, which depends on budget and/or access to institutional resources. So don't stress too much; use what is available for you.

Do you want only your voice with little of the surrounding ambient sound? Then you probably want a cardioid. Not an omni as you'll get too much unwanted background noise, and probably not a shotgun as if you move your head when talking, then you might move out of the mic's pattern. A cardioid is what most people will use for recording themselves at home or in a studio talking.

Do you only have one mic and want to record an interview? Then you'll want a mic with a bi-directional pick-up pattern to get both you and your guest.

Do you want to record voices alongside the environment where you are? Do you want to capture the general sound of a place to paint a picture? Do you want to pin a microphone onto someone's lapel so you can capture their voice without worrying about where they move? Then you'll be looking at an omni. Some radio reporters use these mics to get ambient sound alongside voices. It's the most commonly found pick-up pattern of lapel mics, and your phone or computer.

Do you want to capture a particular voice or sound with little else around? Then you'll want a shotgun. They are often very sensitive to handling noise; they can pick up sounds that you might not want (like a ceiling fan) and can take practice to use well. They are the types of mics you see people using with booms on film sets. They can be really useful for interviewing in noisier places, but need a bit more practice than other mics.

Whatever microphone you use, you will need to learn its specific properties and how they interact with your voice. I know that the mic I can use at the university where I work sounds best when I'm about a fist and a thumb's distance away from it. But I have a deep and loud voice (and a long thumb); for another person it will be different.

A sound wave travels through the air, is picked up by your microphone, and then needs to be recorded. Smartphones and computers can act as reorders (and also both have inbuilt microphones that are probably not very good). Computers and smartphones can be connected to external microphones. There are some pretty decent lapel mics that connect to a phone's headphone jack, whilst many podcasters choose USB mics, especially if they are making a lot of online interviews. There are now many good browser-based podcasting apps that record all sides of the conversation independently and continuously. Not only does it then sound better, but you also get separate files for each speaker, which is great in case, for example, another guest has lots of background noise. I use Squadcast or Zencastr for this, but there are plenty of other options available.

A step up from this is a standalone digital recorder, some of which also act as simple mixing boards specially designed for podcasters. This gives you more control over the sound that comes in, allows you to record multiple sources at once, and is less likely to crash or freeze than a computer. If you are starting out and want to buy gear, then try to buy equipment that allows you to be as flexible as possible, i.e. that allows you to upgrade if you want to. For example, check what type of connection a microphone uses and if it's compatible with your recorder or check if a digital recorder allows for external mics or only has an inbuilt mic, and so on.

Because of the wide variety of equipment available, and because new recorders will be released in the time between me writing these words and the book being published, I won't recommend specific equipment (though Zoom recorders have always served me well). But I do want to emphasise that you should start whatever your budget is. I began podcasting using a second-hand ZoomH2 worth around 30 euros. It's a recorder with a built-in mic. It allowed me to record uni- and bi-directionally as well as capture ambient sound. It can also be plugged into a laptop's USB port and thus act as a USB mic, which I did by plugging it into an old laptop running a Linux-based operating system. My point is:

don't start obsessing about expensive gear if you don't have the funds for it. Rather try to persuade your university to buy expensive stuff and then borrow it or use whatever you can.

Of equal importance as the equipment you can get hold of is the space you use to record. Obviously you want to get rid of unwanted noise in the background, but you also want to pay attention to room acoustics. Even if you've never been in a recording studio you know what they look like – soft and irregular shapes are on the walls to absorb sound and stop sound waves bouncing around. If you want similar acoustics, you can set it up at home or anywhere else using curtains, coats, bed sheets, or wardrobes. Trust your ears and record in different places to see how your and others' voices sound.

Whatever you use to record, you should pay attention to the gain level, so that you're not recording too loud or too quiet. People often ask, 'what level should I set the gain to on my recorder'. The answer is, it depends on how loud the sound source is. If you are recording a voice, then I aim for it to be hitting about −12 and −6 decibels. I usually err on the side of having a lower gain, as it is easy enough to boost quiet recordings using editing software (as long as it's not too quiet), but if a sound is too loud, and peaks past 0 decibels, then it sounds terrible as the sound which was louder than 0 is cut off. People's laughing or screaming is much, much louder than their normal speaking voice.

Record in an uncompressed format. I nearly always record in .wav and I only convert to .mp3 once I finish editing the podcast. Any decent recorder (including browser-based apps, and smartphone apps) should allow you to record in .wav. On half-decent recorders, there is usually the option to change (or at least see) two other settings – sample rate and bit depth. Sample rate refers to the number of times per second the sound source is captured (during conversion from analog to digital) and is measured in Hertz (Hz). The bit depth is the number of bits of information contained within each sample. I usually record at 48,000 Hz 24 bit; 44,100 and 16 bit is also fine.

In these digital times, there is a tendency to record a lot of everything, just think about how many photos you have on your phone. This can be a blessing, because it means we don't have to worry about running out of tape as people did in the past. But it can also be a curse, as it is hard to manage hundreds of hours of recordings, which are much harder to skim than digital photos. When recording, try to keep in mind that someone, most probably you, is going to have to listen to and then edit the recording. If you want a 20-minute interview on a podcast, then try to record a 20-minute interview. It'll probably end up being longer and you'll have to cut it down, but if you record two hours then you'll hate yourself.

You'll also hate yourself if you don't use headphones. Why? Because your microphone picks up sound differently from your ears (see above). If you don't use headphones, then you won't know what it is you are recording, just what your ears hear. You also won't be able to hear any problems your equipment has, for example, maybe there's a buzzing from a mic that's not plugged in properly. I don't care if you think headphones make you look daft, you have to wear them regardless.

Any headphones are better than no headphones. I use studio monitoring headphones so that I hear sound as clean as possible. A lot of headphones nowadays boost the bass in a way that companies think makes music sound better. Avoid these if you can; I find they make the ambient room noise sound much more present than it actually is and also voices sound muddy. In general, though, any headphones should be okay to start out.

What recording advice do other scholar-podcasters have?

00:21:25,000 When we get into the room, I usually turn the recorder on as soon as possible and then just leave it going, which always means that I've got like ten minutes of crap to cut at the beginning. But it means that there's generally not that moment where they go from, 'oh, we're having fun' to 'oh, now I must be serious'. And that helps, I think, to make it run a little more smoothly at the beginning.

Jodie-Lee Trembath, The Familiar Strange

00:16:42,000 I think live should sound live. I mean, there should be some sort of ambient noise. If you're recording on location and you get a bit of restaurant or coffee shop noise around, as long as it's just right, it can be really good. But it is quite challenging at times to get that right.

Dario Llinares, The Cinematologists and
podcast scholar

00:08:53,000 From our own experience of listening to podcasts, it is actually a very forgiving medium. I don't think we don't sound professional, but what sounding professional in a podcast means is quite different from sounding professional in an audio studio. And what I mean by forgiving is that people know you're not Malcolm Gladwell. You know? People know we're not *This American Life*. Because if you listen to an episode from one of those podcasts, you listen to the list of people that they acknowledge at the end who have been part of the production, and there's 25, 30 people who are working on it.

Clare Wright, Archive Fever

00:06:40,000 I think that professionalism really matters. My bachelor's degree is in communications. I had a couple of classes on radio broadcasting, and I was really drawn to public radio. I listened to a tonne of public radio as an undergraduate and I wanted my podcast to sound like that because a lot of the podcasts I'd listen to, I'd be listening in my car or on the train and have to turn it up. And the sound quality was not great, and I didn't want any of that. I felt like that would inhibit people from listening because it was a burden just to make out what people were saying.

Blair Hodges, The Maxwell Institute Podcast

00:13:17,000 One of the coolest things about our show that [co-host] Sam [Clevenger] probably doesn't talk about enough because he's a modest guy, is that he basically produces an album on the theme of the episode. Once we develop a theme Sam will go away and produce a mini album effectively. And then that gives me or Sam a mini library of music to pull from. Which is incredibly useful.

Oliver Rick, Somatic Podcast

00:21:59,000 But you're conscious of sound. Certain things don't translate well to sound and other things are sound gold. And, you know, there are certain things that the mind cannot cognitively process as sound. It's not good sound. So, for instance, I live by the ocean here. The sound of surf is rubbish on tape. It just sounds like white noise. Visually, we need that visual cue to be able to put it together. And that's where all those foley people come in, you know, that clop coconuts together to make the sound of horses. If I want to make the sound of bushfire [makes paper rustling sound], I'll do that. And that will make the sound of crackling of bushfire in the trees. But there are beautiful sounds. That's always sound gold. I literally just grab these sounds anyway as a kind of library of sounds the way that other people take photos.

Siobhan McHugh, documentary podcaster
maker and podcast scholar

Exercise 8 Recording Three Things

Record the following three common podcast elements.

> Narration: Re-record the script you developed in Exercise 5 and refined in Exercise 6.
> Interview: Record an interview based on the questions you developed in Exercise 7.
> Ambient sounds: Capture three different sounds that speak to your podcast topic.

Edit (with flow)

Editing is something which often worries people who have not done it before, but like any craft it can be learnt to greater and lesser degrees. The basics are quite simple to learn, and you'll be able to produce a 'good enough' edit quite quickly. Editing is done in a digital audio workstation (DAW), basically a piece of software for editing audio. When you open any of these up, you might be intimidated by the number of things that it can do. However, do not worry too much about the technical side of things when you first start. It's much more important to think about content, and this essentially involves cutting words and other sounds and moving words and other sounds around, just as you would in a word processer. A lot of people are very sniffy about a free, open-source, and multi-platform DAW called Audacity. I think needlessly so, as it's a great way to learn and make perfectly great simple podcasts.

There are hundreds of online tutorials for the scores of popular DAWs. Those will allow you to deep dive into the technical aspects of specific software and their tools. It does not make too much sense to do this in book format – it is better if you see and hear. And also, honestly, I spent a decade of my life training as an anthropologist, while there are people who spent decades of their lives becoming experts in audio. I can manage okay, but if you want to go deep into editing, follow their YouTube tutorials. In this section, I will talk about a few common mistakes academics I've worked with tend to make and suggest some ways to overcome them when editing a simple podcast (i.e. those podcasts with only voices, some sounds, and intro and outro music, not a richly designed audio documentary).

The most important step in the process of editing is listening to your material. You need to decide which parts of the conversation to keep, which to delete, and whether you want to change the order. This doesn't require any new technical skill; it requires skills scholars already have – editing for clarity and purpose. Don't worry too much about the smaller issues at first, such as coughs or guests restarting their sentences, focus on the big picture. Keep your objective and audience in mind. Pay attention to the content and also how things are being expressed.

Once you're happy with the overall conversation, you'll want to go through the audio and fix all the unwanted sounds. Some people delete all the ums, ahs, mouth/lip noises, breaths, coughs, and so on, and some people leave nearly all of them in. This will depend on what type of podcast you are trying to make. I personally like to leave some of the thinking noises my guests make, but only a few as I want to make them sound even smarter than they already are; nobody really wants to listen to too many ums, and I recognise that being recorded can be an intimidating experience for some, which leads to vocal tics. Be careful when you edit to keep people sounding human. The cadence of people's sentences is important and if you cut out all the gaps between their words then they will sound robotic. If they take very audible breaths and you wish to remove those, then rather than deleting the audio, copy part of the recording where there is no speaking (so that you get the background noise of the recording) and paste it over the breath or other sound, thus keeping the original cadence. It is advisable to record a few seconds of room tone for this (i.e. the sound of the room when no one is talking).

If you have background hiss, computer noise, or other constant unwanted noise, remove it. Every DAW has a noise removal or reduction tool. You need to capture the sound you want removed (from a part where there is no speaking) and apply it to the whole area where the unwanted noise is. But beware if you cut too much, you will also make voices sound unnatural.

Spend some time learning about compression, noise gates, equalisation, and more. Once again, a book is not the place to go into it. You should play around and trust your ears and get happily lost down deep internet rabbit holes where people will discuss and explain everything in such depth your brain will ache.

Finally, remember content is more important than professional sounding editing. This is why I would encourage scholars to edit their own podcasts at least some of the time, or to make sure they have an editor who understands what they are trying to convey.

What do other podcasters have to say about editing?

00:26:08,000 Editing is amazing. It's an invisible art because literally, as I tell my students, the best edit is the inaudible one. If I can even hear a break in tone, that's a bad edit for me. You have to actually get the timing right as well as the word content and the matching tone, so it has to sound natural. But at the same time, you have to be faithful to the rhythms of the voice and to the sort of idiosyncratic expressiveness of the person. I worked with a video editor on one podcast, and he was so used to everything being 'tight, tight, tight, tight' that he completely took out all the little breaths and crutch words that this fellow, a detective, did. And he sounded like a robot. The guy sounded like a robot. It totally dehumanised him. And we had to get them to put them back in. Your focus is otherwise when you're looking at a screen, you're not focused entirely on the voice.

I have this phrase I use a lot, 'you can't freeze frame audio'. Audio only exists in real time. Everything is driven by that, by the beat and the rhythm.

I mean, I love editing. I have a very basic coding method. I just have a log of everything. One column is the time code, one column is key words and content and where I can get out, an actual editable point, and then the other column is reminiscent of kindergarten. They get one star, two stars, or three stars, depending on how good, how strong the content is. And the stuff that gets no stars is never going to get into anything as an audio format. It may contain interesting information, but it will be better digested by me as a narrator.

Siobhan McHugh, documentary podcaster
maker and podcast scholar

00:17:56,000 I did kind of too much editing. Like one episode is on the *Iliad*. I think I spent about eight or ten hours trying to edit just one hour-long episode. Which is too much editing. This erased the natural feel of conversation.

Zhang Zhan, Tianshu

00:44:29,000 What I've noticed is there's a huge amount of power in the actual editing process. If they say something and then go and correct it, you can either edit out the incorrect thing they said or you can leave it in, which would make them sound less of an expert, if that makes sense. There's a lot of control you have in editing the interviewees' file that can make them sound really, really on point, that they never mess up, they never pause for hesitation. Or you can let that stuff in. And that really changes, I think, the impression the listener would have of that person.

Michael Bossetta, Social Media and Politics

00:40:07,000 So I have a bunch of favourite things that I do, tips that I read online. I watched a lot of YouTube videos about audio editing. I read a bunch of podcasting guides. There are some things, very simple things, such as making sure that you get rid of all the background noise. So, you know, if I have a sound like just hitting my microphone by accident, I need to make sure to clip that out. There's also a lot of background noise sometimes and so I know that every time I interview someone, there is this sort of static noise in the background. Knowing how to get an excerpt of that and then cut it from the whole audio all at once is a skill that I had to learn. Things like normalising the decibel that the sound is coming through at is important. Making sure there's a limit as well. When we laugh on the show, when we exclaim something very enthusiastically, there needs to be a limit. So that we're not bursting through people's earphones. So, yeah, there are a lot of tips and tricks.

Michael Rivera, The Arch and Anth Podcast

00:28:25,000 It's pretty bare bones, and deliberately. We try not to kill it by committee. We come up with an idea, we script it, we both record locally. [Audio producer] Claire [Gawne] gets those two audio files. She does lots of line-by-line editing, so we sound more articulate.

From a linguist's perspective, if we're just having a conversation and there's a third person there, that person can influence the conversation by asking questions. We can pay attention to whether they're bored or not. They need pauses to direct what's important when someone's listening to you and they're not present in the conversation, it's the editor's job to do a lot of that work for them. I really like podcasts that take a bit of that friction out of the conversation and thankfully, Claire edits for that. She also will just edit if we get boring. She'll return an episode and be like 'you had three examples, but I cut one because I got bored by the end of it'. She's relentless. A probably related fact is that she's also my sister.

I realised very soon after starting the podcast that as much as I love audio editing, editing a podcast was incompatible with also having a full-time job and my sister had just left a job and I was like, 'you know what you need? You need a new skill set'. I should probably point out at this point in the story, I am her older sister.

Lauren Gawne, Lingthusiasm

Exercise 9 Editing Your Sounds

Using the assembled recordings from Exercise 8, and an online DAW tutorial, put together a simple podcast episode. Export it as an mp3.

Find and Grow (your audience)

Once you have a finished podcast, you need to publish it. For this you need a podcasting host. Different companies offer podcast hosting, but these change all the time so I won't recommend one. At the time of writing, some hosting platforms allow a limited amount of content to be uploaded for free. A podcast hosting service is different from a directory. Your podcast hosting platform will create an RSS feed, which you can then submit to podcast directories (like Apple Podcasts or Spotify), which takes a few days to be approved. These directories also feed the apps on people's smartphones.

When uploading, you'll be asked to submit a podcast description (that you developed above) and 'show notes' for each episode (where you can link to other relevant work, for example). You will also need a logo for your podcast, but remember it will be very small on phone screens.

At this juncture it is worth asking yourself, again, why you are making your podcast and who you are making it for. To speak to a community of scholars? To speak to students or potential students of your discipline? To speak to people from a different discipline but who work on the same topic?

Do not get too stressed about numbers, especially at the beginning. Although there are a few scholarly podcasts with large numbers, most independent podcasters I spoke with for this book were getting between 200 and 700 downloads per episode, and those numbers took a while to build up. In the beginning, you might only get a handful of listeners until you manage to establish your podcast. You need to be consistent, but you also need to find your audience. You should have already defined your audience before starting, but remind yourself, and think about how to reach this audience once the podcast is made.

If you set up a Twitter account and tweet 'new podcast up' nobody will respond. Social media is both a time suck and dependent on relationship building. If you are going to maintain Twitter, Facebook, and Instagram accounts (to name just the most popular at the time of writing), then you will have to pump a lot of hours into it on a regular basis. These companies' business models are built on getting people to spend as much time as possible on the sites. They reward those who spend a lot of time creating content by allowing their content to be seen more widely. Moreover, different platforms require different approaches; *The People's Scientist* a.k.a. Stephanie Caligiuri creates TikTok-style dances for her episodes.

If you are creating a relatively niche podcast, then you are going to want to be able to find that audience and build relationships with them. Social media might work for this, for example, if you have potential listeners who are very active around the topic or theme of your podcast, but you might also just be posting into the void, generating a few engagements on your post and from people who might never listen to your podcast. Your personal social media handles may already have a lot of relevant followers, and it might be just as useful to post there as it would be to create new podcast specific accounts (however, if you make a podcast specific to your field a lot of your 'friends' might 'like' it, but how many of them would listen to more than a few minutes?). Some universities have social media teams that promote the work of faculty and students, whilst some only post asinine PR about the university and the 'brilliance' of its senior leadership. If you're lucky enough to work in a university that actively promotes its faculty and student research, then you can reach out to them about how best to work together.

Within and beyond social media, you need to think about where your audience is and how to reach them. Maybe it's a particular academic listserv, maybe it's a particular university department of professional society. If so, then you need to think about how you access these spaces in a way that is useful for audience building but does not annoy those who rely on those lists for information. Maybe the largest professional society in your field is conservative and would never post anything about a podcast unless it already featured the biggest names in the field? But maybe that's fine because you wouldn't want to be associated with them anyway. If there are conferences filled with potential listeners then they might be good places for posters, postcards, and other forms of offline promotion. You can also ask your podcast guests to promote the podcast themselves, which opens the door to new groups of potential listeners.

Certain episodes will get more attention than others, but the key to building a sustainable podcast is developing a core audience of subscribers. People who not only listen to one episode but multiple, who interact with the podcast, who tell others about it, who allow you to try new things together. The technology of podcasting is built exactly for this, i.e. on the subscription model. Putting a standalone piece of audio up online is not really a podcast, a podcast is something that people can subscribe to.

The directories where people find your podcast, be they Apple Podcasts or Spotify or whatever, do not host the actual audio files, but the apps people have on their phones draw from these directories, and so it is vital to get your podcast into as many of these as possible. First, you need to find a podcasting hosting service. Most of these you have to pay for, but there are a few that offer free services if you only post a limited amount of content a month. Some universities will offer this service to their staff and students. You cannot just upload the audio file to a website, because then you will not be able to get it into the podcast directories. Podcast hosting sites allow you to generate a feed that can then be found within directories and subscribed to.

You will have some potential listeners within the academic community who are not comfortable with smartphones or technology in general. To be as accessible as possible, you might also want to run a good old-fashioned email subscription, upload your podcasts onto YouTube, and maintain a website where all of the podcasts can be found (you will be able to embed a podcast player from your hosting service or just upload it).

How have others developed their audience?

> 00:10:09,000 So we started out with about 1500 people, and that was just people that already knew about *The Maxwell Institute* that I work at, and that really are these Mormon intellectual type of people that are invested in the life of the mind. I would say, it even has a religious value to them. So, we had this core audience of people that was interested, about 1500. And then I would invite them to share the podcast. I did Facebook ads, had a Twitter presence, and would encourage word of mouth, things like that. And then I would reach out to universities, because I didn't want it originally to be a show for Mormons. The whole goal was for it to be about religion in general. Personally, for me, I'm a Mormon and I wanted my co-religionists

to start thinking more critically about religion and to learn more about other religions. And so, I would reach out when I would have a guest who did something on the Koran. I would send that to Facebook groups like *Islam in the Academy*. So, I would send links to them, I would invite all my guests, I would send them promo stuff like 'put this on your Facebook', 'send this to your students', 'here's all the links'. I would make it easy for them. All you have to do is copy this and send it out to your email list. And so over time, I pulled our audience. After about three years, we were averaging about 5–6000 downloads an episode, and as it turned out, we were like 60 percent non-Mormon to 40 percent Mormon, which shocked me.

The bigger and bigger guests I got I would notice a considerable uptick. I got this guy named Pete Enns who's a really popular former evangelical Bible scholar and his episode just exploded, like 25,000 downloads in the first week, cause he sent it out to his mailing list and then you'd probably retain like five or ten percent of those and start to get residual downloads. And so that's how the audience has built up.

And then I've also found that getting ratings and reviews on Apple podcasts makes a big difference. I would do little gimmicks. Like I started reading a review of the month. During every episode, I'd be like, 'hey, so here's our review of the month from Joey Jo-Jo. And here's what they said'. People want to hear their names. So, I found that, like when I did that, I would get two or three reviews every episode.

I just found ways to promote it through the scholars who were on the show, through me going to universities, in Facebook groups and in places like that, sending links to people when I think an episode would matter to them, and having my audience share it.

Blair Hodges, The Maxwell Institute Podcast

01:07:17,000 People will often say that podcast listeners' statistics are unreliable or distorted or something like this. This is not an uncommon problem in the media generally. I mean, when I worked at *The Atlantic*, I used to think of *The Atlantic* as a machine. It wasn't a magazine, it was a machine that produced guilt because we knew for a fact that lots of people subscribe to it and just looked at it like, 'I should read that, I really should. But I don't have time. So, I'm gonna put it on my coffee table and I'm going to worry about not reading it. I'm going to feel guilty about not reading it'.

Marshall Poe, New Books Network

The first thing was that we knew we needed a strategy, a social media strategy, a public outreach strategy. The second thing was that [co-host] Ian [Pollock] and I then went and did an eight-week course to upskill on how to promote a blog or podcast. So that was invaluable. And then and through that, we had assessments that we had to do. And it ended with us having to put together a full social media strategy for the projects which the four of us did together. And so that helped. And then it was kind of a matter of implementing it.

Jodie-Lee Trembath, The Familiar Strange

00:15:53,000 You know, a lot of listeners are never going to set foot on your campus, but I think that's OK. And I think that's the mindset that academia really needs to start to work through, like reconceiving what the university's role is in society more broadly. We have all this expertise, we have the ability to do this. I feel really lucky that I don't have to go out and chase advertisers and do all these things. How can we think about education as a public good? How can we use podcasts as a delivery method for that? A listener doesn't care if it's from Penn State, or the University of California, or Harvard, or some private liberal arts college that they've never heard of, or somewhere outside the US. They're really content focused, not institution focused, which is not the way that academia operates at all.

Jenna Spinelle, Democracy Works

00:02:46,000 It's important to have the consistency, whether you decide to have a weekly format or not, but to have a trustable, predictable schedule, whether that's every other week, every day, twice a day. That really works, both in terms of your audience, the people, but also in terms of the algorithms. And some of this is behind the black box, so you don't quite know how they're working, but sometimes you're able to glean things.

Bonni Stachowiak, Teaching in Higher Ed

00:53:43,000 I think people see the technology and don't realise that it's mostly about human connection. It's about community more than anything. Having a community of listeners is a weird and cool thing.

Dave Brodbeck, Spit and Twitches

00:20:22,000 It all comes back to thinking about your audience. This is what I tell my students: podcasting, like all media, is a relationship. It's not audio in the same way that photography isn't ink on paper, and in the same way that TV isn't pixels on a screen. It is a relationship that you create. And in order to enter that dance, to have that kind of relationship with someone, you have to know who you're dancing with and you have to know what steps they know, and what might thrill them. And without that understanding, you're really going to struggle.

Martin Spinelli, podcast scholar

00:44:01,000 We have been thinking perhaps more substantively about reactions when we were making the podcast. And of course, we deal with incredibly politically sensitive issues like genocide, which of course is a highly-contested issue because it's a crime, it's a historical phenomenon, and there's people who have suffered it and people who have perpetrated it. And of course, we also made an episode about colonial crimes. Our country, like yours, has a colonial history which has not been dealt with properly in different communities and can spark some reaction in other communities. But in the end, we never got any negative reaction. I think we spent more time thinking about what the dangers were rather than the reactions that we got.

Thijs Bouwknegt, NIOD Rewind Podcast on War & Violence

00:52:10,000 I think a bad academic podcast is when you didn't figure out your public. If you decide to make an academic podcast for the general public and you choose all of these channels to distribute it and then you stick to interviewing very academic people who don't realise they're talking to non-specialists, that's a recipe for disaster. Or if you make a very light-hearted loose discussion type of podcast and then you just distribute it amongst your academic peers. I mean, it might work, but then why wouldn't you open it to a larger public?

Dumitrița Holdiș, Down, but Not Out

00:51:24,000 It's counterintuitive. People who want to reach different publics should get even more specific about the person, not the people, but the person that they want to most reach. And that will permeate the noise because there is so much noise. Everyone has a podcast today. And the other thing that will permeate that noise is the consistency. My husband and I have both decided that we will never be able to produce perfect podcasts. If you think the goal is every single week, there's going to be some that you think are amazing and other people think are just all right. And then there's some that really resonate with other people, and you're like, 'oh, I just thought that one was okay'. So just being okay with 'good enough' is such a valuable lesson in podcasting, but also in life in general.

Bonni Stachowiak, Teaching in Higher Ed

00:16:36,000 When we launched it, we also had this public event with a live discussion. And then we thought of recording events to build a community around these discussions. To make the podcast, and grow the possible audience. We did seven or eight live events.

Maria Martelli, contrasens

00:32:12,000 We very quickly realised that if the show was going to keep going, the only way it was going to keep going is if it was run on a profit model. And we very quickly decided that advertising wasn't going to be our vibe, partly because that required us growing the show a bit more in those initial months where we only had a few thousand listeners. But also, it's just it's kind of a tricky thing to balance.

So we looked to the Patreon model, and that's worked really well for us. Not because of anything secret, we literally just went and studied ten Patreon pages for podcasts we liked and we replicated what worked. We found that the ones that were doing well had a relatively equal amount of bonus content to their free content that was somewhere at the four to eight dollar level of support per month. And that's the model we emulated. And we used that to ramp up slowly.

It was only once we'd made the bare minimum money to pay [my sister] Claire, who was also doing transcripts and not necessarily enjoying it at the time.

And we definitely weren't paying her commercial rates for any of that work. It was only once we were paying her enough to do both a main episode and a bonus that we moved to full length bonus episodes as well. So we deliberately built in growth into that model. And now the show pays Claire to edit both the main and the bonus every month, as well as do about 20 hours of admin over that month, because as the show grows, and now there are about 700 patrons, we have to do a lot of management there.

We also started running merchandise, which Claire helps with, which is another fun skill set I didn't think I'd have a few years ago, but I quite like. And then we also pay our transcriptionists commercial rates and, yes, the show pays us an amount. Definitely not an amount that offsets enough for me to stop working. But it allows us to do things, like we're running a programme called the *LinComm Grants* where we're funding three 500-dollar grants for interesting linguistics communication projects. So, we see the money that the show makes as a way to continue to build community.

Lauren Gawne, Lingthusiasm

00:08:11,000 I strongly believe that it is necessary to have podcasts be as accessible as possible, and even personally there are times I don't want to listen to an entire podcast, but I want to know what it was about and the gist of what was said, and I get so frustrated when I look for a transcript and there isn't one. From the very beginning, we have had a transcript that appears at the same time as every episode. When we started, I transcribed it all, just listening to it and typing, I now put it in to an A.I. assisted automatic transcript thing and then go clean it up, which takes actually not that much less time, but it's somehow much less tiring. I do that and it takes me two to three times the length of an episode to make a transcript. And I feel like it's a small price to pay to have it be accessible.

I've heard from deaf and hard of hearing people that they really appreciate that it has a transcript, which was the reason that I was motivated to do that in the first place. But I've also heard from hearing people who just prefer reading to listening and people who aren't native English speakers, that it's easier for them to digest it if they have a transcript to look at.

It's not just good for being accessible, but it makes it searchable later, which is so valuable. And it can be so frustrating when you're listening to a podcast, you're like, 'oh, that was a great quote. I was cooking dinner while I was listening to it. Where was it in the podcast?' And you just can't find it. Or like, 'when did they talk about this? I want to look up the name of that book that they mentioned' or whatever, and you can't find it. And having it be searchable, I think, is really valuable for academics.

Evelyn Lamb, My Favorite Theorem

00:54:11,000 One thing I do wonder about, and worry about a little bit, that we haven't really talked about, is the ephemerality, like the possible disappearance. Like where are these podcasts?

Let's say I stopped being at the institute and someone came in and didn't want to pay a monthly hosting fee? I have backups of all my episodes, but, I don't know if I would have the money or time to go post them up some place. Are they going to disappear? Transcripts help with accessibility, but I do wonder a little bit about the transient nature of online materials, like there's been a few podcast episodes from old shows where I was looking somebody up and was like, 'oh, they did a podcast interview like seven years ago' and go look at this, and I couldn't find the audio file, it just wasn't there anymore and what a bummer that was. So, I think that's one interesting thing – how sturdy is it as a medium? And that depends on money and time and interest of the person who posted it.

Blair Hodges, The Maxwell Institute Podcast

00:26:23,000 I think if we were well indexed, for example, that could help, too. So, if I want to see all the podcasts on influenza viruses or whatever, that could help. But we don't because we don't have enough time to do that.

Vincent Racaniello, This Week in Virology

00:04:56,000 I think how we approached doing the podcast *Preserves* had to do a lot with our overall goals. We wanted to develop a podcast series since it was accessible to the public but still grounded in good academic practice and student involvement.

We wanted to make sure that we would do podcasts, kind of like an essay in which they would all be transcribed and footnoted heavily. So, we would always have a source page, I feel that that's one of the things that's missing in academia. We want this podcast to be a way into further research and not just be the one thing or the one argument that's out there. We want to make sure that people can access those kinds of sources.

Kent Davies, Preserves and podcast instructor

Exercise 10 Publishing

Choose a podcast hosting service. Upload your podcast, description, and logo. Submit it to all the popular directories. Then let your potential audience know about your podcast. Don't stop podcasting.

Change (our institutional practices)

If you are going to start podcasting seriously, then it's going to take up a considerable amount of your time. No matter what your day job is, you're going to have to find a way to fit it into your scholarly practice. You can call it a hobby, a key component of your work, a research tool, a means of networking, a way to change academia, or whatever you like but because it is different to 'traditional' scholarly practice (and new-ish), it entails a different way of being a scholar. Others, including those individuals and institutions who do not podcast or maybe those who do not even understand why or what scholars podcast, will define your practice whether you like it or not. You may not be able to completely control how podcasting is conceived or materially rewarded by others, but you can at least think about how you define it in relation to your wider intellectual labour, whether you're a researcher, a professor, a student, a teacher, a publicly engaged practitioner, an enthusiastic amateur, or anything else. This change will have to be both an individual and collective undertaking.

How have scholars who podcast worked with and through institutional norms and structures?

> 00:01:07,000 We went along to our first ever academic conference at the same time, [co-host] David [G. Robertson] and I, to the British Association for the Study of Religions [BASR]. We thought, 'there's going to be a lot of scholars there. I'm sure we can maybe get a few of them just talking to us'. We prearranged two and then, in the course of that two-day conference, another three people were like, 'fine, yeah, speak to me' and everyone in the committee of the association and everything, were just like, 'this is a great idea. It's great to see such enthusiasm. This is fantastic!' That was in September, but by the time we launched the podcast publicly in January, the British Association got in touch and said, 'look, you know, we can't give you any money just now, but, you know, we'd be happy to lend you a sort of institutional support'.
>
> So right from the beginning, it was the Religious Studies Project presented in association with the British Association for the Study of Religions, which really just gave us an excellent legitimation in that sense, we're not just doing this on our own, we've got the support of an academic community. And then that, within

a year, turned into, 'you're doing great work, guys. We probably can give you some money' and that support has continued from the get-go. And I suppose once one association got involved, some others wanted to get involved, too. We've always kept the BASR close to our heart and their name always comes first on the list of sponsors, because they've been with us since day one.

We've also then, sort of, become an institution. I mean, we're here, alongside all these existing scholarly bodies, and obviously being supported by them, but we've always wanted to keep ourselves aloof and not become too institutionalised.

Chris Cotter, The Religious Studies Project

00:27:42,000 In terms of institutional support, I think we are quite lucky in that our institutions do support us. My Dean and my Pro-Vice-Chancellor of Research they follow the podcast and they know what we do and I get commended on this. They do think that this is really important, that we talk about our research and that this is a great thing to do. And they put this as an exemplar thing of what other academics should be striving to do. I do appreciate that, actually, we are quite lucky in that sense.

Ksenia Chmutina, Disasters Deconstructed

00:28:28,000 And then there's universities themselves that can try and control quality. I know University College London [UCL] is trying to do this now. They're trying to sort of create certain standards for all the different podcasts that come out of the university. Now, I'm a bit scared about that because, right now, there's no reason that it has to be associated with University College London, even though I work there. And so that's going to be a tricky balance for us because we want to be in partnership with UCL, but we don't want to be controlled by them.

And that comes to this bigger point of content control. And, you know, the moment you start adding in quality checks, it depends on who's checking it and whose interests they have in mind. And so, for instance, you know, we've had people that have come up to us and say, 'yes, we want you to put together a podcast and we'll give you some money to do it'. And in a sense, I think of that as sponsored content and the quality would be checked by them, of course, right. Making sure that it lives up to their interests, whatever they are. And so, I had a conversation with my board very early on and we basically said, 'we're not doing that. We won't take any money to make sponsored content'. And subsequently, all of our funders have basically agreed that we have total creative control over the show. So, we won't take anyone's money if they want to basically tell us how to edit.

Will Brehm, FreshEd

00:27:57,000 One of the most basic problems of podcasting, especially academic podcasting, is finding a way to support it financially. This has been the biggest challenge for me on the *New Books Network*. It was really not a huge problem for me to go from a few thousand listeners to a few hundred thousand listeners. But it's been a huge problem getting anyone to pay for it.

Marshall Poe, New Books Network

00:44:30,000 My concern is that there's a lot of public knowledge creation that's going on that is being slotted into a service capacity. I think that people who are writing regularly on respectable blogs are doing knowledge creation in a way that is parallel to, in lots of ways, a peer-reviewed traditional journal article. And podcasting, if it's taking on some of the same sort of preparations, if you have to do scholarly research to create a podcast discussion or a conversation, then you're doing the same kind of research that you would be doing if you were writing a journal article. And that not everything that isn't a journal article format should be considered service. And that's why I keep using the terminology 'knowledge creation' because I think that's really important. And that's what the traditional peer review is about: knowledge creation. But does knowledge creation happen outside of traditional peer-reviewed book or articles? I think that it does, and I think that we are in a moving landscape with regard to it.

Lilly Goren, New Books in Political Science

00:53:22,000 I would love it if academic podcasting was genuinely changing anthropology and was the kind of thing that would contribute, to sound selfish, making people's careers, because the reality is, that it takes a lot of time and a lot of work and a lot of editing goes into making all the episodes.

Simon Theobald, The Familiar Strange

00:06:22,000 I said that there is something complimentary about conventional academic knowledge production and podcasting. But there is also something competing. Given the limited amount of time that I have available to produce things as a researcher, the time that I put in for podcasting is time that I don't put in for publishing papers or books. There is this competition that I also need to figure out myself. How much weight do I give one or the other? There's this big seduction that I do more podcasting than I should.

Markus Kip, Urban Political Podcast

00:47:42,000 This is my personal podcasting soapbox. The real reason why I'm invested in things like peer review and tenure and promotion committees is that podcasting is one of many forms of publicly engaged and accessible scholarship that scholars are interested in working on, and the scholars who are always thinking about publicly engaged and accessible scholarship are minoritised scholars: queer, working class, black, indigenous, people of colour, disabled scholars. These are the ones who come into the university with a sense of accountability and responsibility to communities out-side of the university, who are going to do work for those communities, whether or not it's valued. And across the board, what that means is that they end up doing twice the work, that they're doing all of this account-able, accessible, community-engaged scholarship and then they also have to do all of the other stuff that looks 'real' to the university. So, podcasting for me, particu-larly doing this larger infrastructure, capacity-building work around the edges of podcasting, is an equity issue.

Hannah McGregor, Secret Feminist Agenda and podcast scholar

00:50:01,000 I think one thing that I keep circling around to in conversations with colleagues who are completely mystified by podcasting, but also with colleagues who are also deeply involved in podcast-ing, is that there is a lot of energy expended worrying about 'impact' and 'engagement' and not a lot of time spent articulating exactly what our concerns are over those things. I started the podcast when I was in the U.K. The REF [Research Excellence Framework] is a never-ending nightmare in terms of the emotional toll it exacts on people. Not even really thinking about the logistical toll it exerts on people. And in Australia, we're currently in the grip of a similar set of anxieties and, I think, one thing that podcasting has done has made me very aware of the importance of thinking about these things and articulating ways in which we are engaging with people and finding ways to express that. But I think it's frustrating to still have universi-ties be obsessed with the traditional publication model when the podcast does sometimes far more interesting things than my academic publications ever will.

I think I don't actually care that much about the university's models of impact and engagement. I care about thinking about it for my own sake because it's really the question of why I am doing this.

Lauren Gawne, Lingthusiasm

5   The Next Episode

What next for scholarly podcasting?

> Step into my dream. A dream with two seemingly contradictory but actually productively contrasting strands: the formalisation and generative wildness of scholarly podcasting futures...
>
> ...podcasts are fully transcribed, making it easy for academics to cite and quote them...
>
> ...podcasts are indexed, catalogued, easily navigable, and subscribable by topic, theme, producer, guest...
>
> ...podcasts are open for collaborative annotation with time-stamped marginalia engendering debate and discussion...
>
> ...attempts to turn podcasts into nothing more than their transcripts fail...
>
> ...attempts to apply the same review processes to podcasts as to texts fail...
>
> ...attempts to establish conventions of form and structure similar to much academic writing fail...
>
> ...the ongoing recognition of scholarly podcasts as legitimate scholarly work leads to an initial dampening of the craft's creative edge, but scholars move to other avenues in search of expression...
>
> ...more and more degree programmes offer 'digital media skills' as options so as to sell 'increased employability' to their student-customers...

DOI: 10.4324/9781003006596-5

...there is a demand for those who teach how to translate intellectual concerns into podcasts...

...younger generations believe that their digital media practices can be transformed into legitimate scholarship...

...the communities formed by podcasting scholars develop in unforeseen ways, suggesting generous ways of producing scholarship and intellectual engagement outside universities...

...a wider acceptance of non-textual forms of knowledge creation and publishing brings scholarly podcasting and other forms of digital media into more regular and sustained dialogue...

...traditional sources of legitimation and authority continue to break down, but scholars don't retreat into their towers wagging their citation count at the plebs as they retreat, but open up and take the time to explain their methods, reasons, and arguments...

...scholars seek new forms of evaluation, finding ways to weave legitimacy and transparency into their podcasting practices...

... and thus podcasting-as-scholarship is no longer just a claim by some, but a dream for all.

Annexes

List of Podcasters Interviewed

Podcast	Podcasters	Disciplines/ Topics	Country
A History of Central Florida	Robert Cassanello	History	U.S.A.
Acadammit Podcast	Place + Space Collective: Diandra Oliver, Samantha Thompson, Trevor Wideman	Geography	Canada
Arch and Anth Podcast	Michael Rivera	Archaeology, Anthropology	Hong Kong
Archive Fever	Claire Wright, Yves Rees	History	Australia
Audiopi's Sociology	Laura Pountney	Sociology	U.K.
Big Biology	Marty Martin, Art Woods	Biology	U.S.A.
BredowCast	Johanna Sebauer	Media Studies	Germany
Brexit Brits Abroad	Michaela Benson	Sociology	U.K.
The Cinematologists	Dario Llinares, Neil Fox	Film Studies	U.K.
City Road Podcast	Dallas Rogers	Urban Studies	Australia

(*Continued*)

Podcast	Podcasters	Disciplines/ Topics	Country
Coffee & Cocktails	Ann Wand	General	U.K.
contrasens	Maria Martelli, Marina Mironica	Sociology	Romania
Cultures of Energy	Cymene Howe, Dominic Boyer	Anthropology, Environmental Sciences	U.S.A.
Democracy Works	Jenna Spinelle	Democracy	U.S.A.
Disasters Deconstructed Podcast	Ksenia Chmutina, Jason von Meding	Disaster Studies	U.K., U.S.A.
Distillations	Mariel Carr	Science History	U.S.A.
Down, but Not Out	Dumitriţa Holdiş	Media Studies	Hungary
EH Out Loud	Krista Caballero	Humanities	U.S.A.
Energy and Innovation	Michael LaBelle	Business Studies, Environmental Sciences	Austria
In Common	Stefan Partelow, Michael E Cox	Sustainability	Germany, U.S.A.
FreshEd	Will Brehm	Higher Education	U.K.
Fully Automated	Nicholas Kiersey	Political Science	U.S.A.
Ganatantra	Sarayu Natarajan, Alok Prasanna Kumar	Politics	India
Global Development Primer	Robert Huish	Development Studies	Canada
Hardcore History	Dan Carlin	History	U.S.A.
Heart of Artness	Siobhan McHugh	Aboriginal art	Australia
Higher Education, Human Employment	Heather May Morgan	Postgraduate Study and Employability	U.K.
History of Philosophy Without Any Gaps	Peter Adamson	Philosophy, History	Germany
How to Build a Stock Exchange: Making Finance Fit for the Future	Philip Roscoe	Management	U.K.
In Defense of Plants	Matt Candeias	Plants, Biology	U.S.A.
In Theory	Maria Sachiko Cecire	Social Theory	U.S.A.

(*Continued*)

Podcast	Podcasters	Disciplines/ Topics	Country
Ipse Dixit	Brian L. Frye	Legal Studies	U.S.A.
Mundaréu	Soraya Fleischer	Anthropology	Brazil
My Favorite Theorem	Evelyn Lamb, Kevin Knudson	Mathematics	U.S.A.
New Books Network	Marshall Poe	All	Everywhere
New Books in Political Science	Lilly Goren	Political Science	U.S.A.
NIOD Rewind Podcast on War & Violence	Anne van Mourik, Thijs Bouwknegt	War, Violence, History	Netherlands
PhDivas Podcast	Liz Wayne, Christine Yao	Academia, Culture, Social Justice	U.S.A., U.K.
PhDrinking	Sadie Witkowski	Mixed	U.S.A.
Podlog	Moritz Klenk	Cultural Sciences	Germany
Preserves	Kent Davies	Oral History, Food	Canada
Public Lands Podcast	Mark Pedelty	Public Land	U.S.A.
SRB Podcast	Sean Guillory	Area Studies, Russia	U.S.A.
Secret Feminist Agenda	Hannah McGregor	Gender Studies	Canada
Sexuality and Gender in Turkey	Mert Koçak	Gender Studies	Turkey
Social Media and Politics	Michael Bossetta	Political Science, Media Studies	Sweden
Somatic Podcast	Oliver Rick, Samuel M. Clevenger	the body in motion	U.S.A.
Spit and Twitches: The Animal Cognition Podcast	Dave Brodbeck	Animal Cognition	Canada
State of the Theory Podcast	Anindya Raychaudhuri, Hannah Fitzpatrick	Social Theory, Pop Culture	U.K.
STEMS and Leaves	Ezra Mattaridi	Science, technology, engineering, and mathematics	U.S.A.

(*Continued*)

Podcast	Podcasters	Disciplines/ Topics	Country
Talking Indonesia	Jemma Purdey, Dave McRae	Area Studies, Indonesia	Australia
Teaching in Higher Ed	Bonni Stachowiak	Higher Education	U.S.A.
The Annex Sociology Podcast	Joseph Cohen	Sociology	U.S.A.
The Anthill	Annabel Bligh	Mixed	U.K.
The Cosmic Savannah	Jacinta Delhaize, Daniel Cunnama	Astronomy	South Africa
The Convivial Conservation Podcast	Judith Krauss	Conservation	U.K.
The Familiar Strange	Julia Brown, Jodie-Lee Trembath, Ian Pollock, Simon Theobald	Anthropology	Australia
The Human Show	Corina Enache	Anthropology	The Netherlands
The Maxwell Institute Podcast	Blair Hodges	Religious Studies	U.S.A.
The Migration Podcast	Fiona Seiger	Migration Studies	The Netherlands
The Naked Scientists	Chris Smith	Natural Science, General Science	U.K.
The Nature Podcast	Nick Howe, Benjamin Thompson	Natural Science	U.K.
The Panpsycast	Jack Symes	Philosophy	U.K.
The People's Scientist	Stephanie Caligiuri	Neuroscience, Physiology, and Nutrition	U.S.A.
The Religious Studies Project	Chris Cotter	Religious Studies	U.K.
The Sources of the Nile	Emanuele Fantini, Emilie Buist	Media Studies	Netherlands
The Vocal Fries	Carrie Gillon	Linguistics	U.S.A.
This Week in Evolution	Vincent Racaniello	Evolution	U.S.A.

(*Continued*)

Podcast	Podcasters	Disciplines/ Topics	Country
This Week in Microbiology	Vincent Racaniello	Microbiology	U.S.A.
This Week in Parasitism	Vincent Racaniello	Parasitism	U.S.A.
This Week in Virology	Vincent Racaniello	Virology	U.S.A.
Tianshu	Zhang Zhan	History, Philology	U.S.A.
Urban Political Podcast	Markus Kip	Urban Studies, Politics	Germany, U.K.
Världar i Omställning/ Worlds in Transition	Maria Ehrnström-Fuentes	Sustainability	Finland
What the If?	Philip Shane, Matt Stanley	Science, Science Fiction, Biology, Physics, Evolution, Space Travel, Engineering, Astronomy	U.S.A.
York Crime Walk	Matt Coward-Gibbs	Sociology	U.K.
York Death & Culture Walk	Matt Coward-Gibbs	Sociology	U.K.

Podcast Scholars and Teachers
Lori Beckstead
Richard Berry
Kent Davies
Alyn Euritt
Kim Fox
Neil Fox
Dario Llinares
Siobhan McHugh
Hannah McGregor
Martin Spinelli

Course Podcast Example Assignment

Prepare a 15–20-minute-long audio podcast in which you interview a professional/academic/practitioner/'real person' about their thoughts on _____ with a special emphasis on _____. You will receive training and on-going support in developing the podcast.

There will be an opportunity to publish podcasts____.

Suggested elements of the podcast:

* Intro and context – circa 500–800 words of scripted narration that introduces the issue and concept(s) you are addressing (2–3 min).
* Edited interview OR narrative + soundscapes OR group discussion (10–15 minutes after editing).
* Analysis and synthesis, scripted argumentation (3–5 minutes).

Additional mandatory material (to be submitted in writing):

* Full reference list, including all the sources used regardless of medium (articles, video documentary, speeches, archives sound bites, and so on – should be referenced and linked if possible).
* Your personal reflections on creating the podcast.

Challenges you might face:

* You will need to spend some time to learn the technology, including recording devices and editing software. You will receive the necessary training during the course, but you will need to allocate some time to practice your new skills.

- You might be tempted to spend too much time preparing the recording.
- Plan in advance, and book the studio/equipment when you need it.

<u>Embedding in the course:</u>

Podcasting is relevant to the course because _____.

<u>Structure and Scaffolding</u>

Which session?	*Podcast progress*	*Deliverable*
Week 1	Introduction to course, explaining podcast assignment. Ask students to come to the first class with a possible topic or person to interview in mind.	
Week 2	Session on learning how to podcast: interviewing, writing for the ear, editing, recording	Task 1: Edited audio file for editing assignment
Week 3	Working on podcast project proposal: identify whom you would like to interview, and what topic you would like to discuss with them	
Week 4–5	Submitting podcast proposal	Task 2: Draft project proposal specifying topic, research question, bibliography, and selected interviewee(s) and concrete questions – this might be considered as the midterm exam

(Continued)

Which session?	*Podcast progress*	*Deliverable*
Week 5	Preparing interview questions Setting up interview time	
Week 6–8	Recording	
Week 8	Drafting analysis	Task 3: Interview audio file and draft script of written analysis
Week 9–10	Recording contextualisation and analysis and editing podcast	
Week 11–12	Final submission	Task 4: Podcast and accompanying reference list, possibly additional material for publishing
Week 13–14	Feedback and fine-tuning session (and publishing if of sufficient quality)	

Assessment Rubrics

The podcast will count for __% of the final grade. You will get __% credit for attending the training and submitting all the interim deliverables as listed above. These will be evaluated on a pass/fail basis.

Description of assignment:

	Excellent	Competent	Developing
Technical production (pass/fail): Make sure one can listen to the podcast and aim to make it a pleasure to listen to it	Appropriate length, audible narration, and interviews, aiming for equal levels throughout the podcast, proper grammar, and plain English. Music and other sounds are appropriately used to further understanding.		
Structure and language – writing, speaking, and listening (30%): Make sure the podcast includes all necessary elements and uses plain English	The podcast has a story to tell; it is written for the ear and is told in an engaging fashion in *plain English*. The podcast catches the listener's attention and builds the complexity of the issue step by step. Its introduction describes the problem area and asks a question that the podcast aims to answer. It explains all concepts that are used in the podcast's interview and analysis and gives necessary background information about the place and topic, whilst also sharing the significance of the interviewee. The interview has a storyline, the questions build on the answers. The interview demonstrates active listening and includes critical questions to the interviewee. The analysis, building on the introduction and the interview, integrates data, interview, and literature and provides a critical overview of the topic.	The podcast has a clear structure and is easy to follow. It explains concepts clearly in the introduction. Its language is clear, it uses plain English, it is brief and avoids complicated vocabulary. The interview revolves around the topic of the podcast, and shows some degree of active listening, but the questions are sometimes jumping between issues and do not exhibit the characteristics of a natural conversation. The questions fail to prompt critical responses from the interviewee.	The podcast includes all required elements but has a fragmented structure, without a clear storyline. Its language is complicated with long sentences and scientific terminology. The bridges and explanations between sections are often missing. The interview questions are sometimes outside of the context; there is no active listening; and the interview does not feel like a natural conversation but rather like answers to a survey.

(Continued)

Description of assignment:

	Excellent	Competent	Developing
Link to concepts in class (30%): Ensure the podcast is relevant to one or more concepts discussed during class	The podcast *critically* examines and links several concepts discussed in class and builds upon the ideas and insights of the interviewee. The interview challenges the interviewee to think critically about the topic being discussed.	The podcast builds upon more than one concept discussed in class and can bridge between the concepts.	The podcast links to one or more concepts discussed in class but could benefit from more analysis and critical thinking.
Synthesis, integration, critical analysis (40%): Step one step back and link all parts of the podcast together: synthesise and contextualise	The podcast shows evidence of deeper critical thinking about the topic. It bridges and critically examines data, the interviewee's answers, and the concepts discussed in class. The podcast clearly demonstrates critical thinking and argumentation skills.	The podcast demonstrates analytical skills and describes the bigger picture; however, it fails to provide a critical insight into the topic.	The podcast lacks analysis and only paraphrases the interview. It fails to provide an analytical or critical overview of the topic.

Note: this rubric is based on one developed by Márta Vetier. Thanks to Emanuele Fantini for his helpful comments around active listening.

Bibliography

Abdous, M'hammed, Betty Rose Facer, and Cherng-Jyh Yen. 2012. 'Academic Effectiveness of Podcasting: A Comparative Study of Integrated versus Supplemental Use of Podcasting in Second Language Classes'. *Computers & Education* 58 (1): 43–52. doi: 10.1016/j.compedu.2011.08.021.

Alegi, Peter. 2012. 'Podcasting the Past: Africa Past and Present and (South) African History in the Digital Age'. *South African Historical Journal* 64 (2): 206–20. doi: 10.1080/02582473.2011.640344.

Altvater, Fran. 2009. 'Words on the Wadsworth: Podcasting and the Teaching of Art History'. *The Journal of Effective Teaching* 9 (3): 12.

Barker, Philip W., Suzanne M. Chod, and William J. Muck. 2020. 'Political Science, Public Intellectualism, and Podcasting'. *PS: Political Science & Politics* 53 (2): 326–7. doi: 10.1017/S104909651900163X.

Barnes, Jared, Candis Carraway, and Stephanie Jones. n.d. 'Using Lecture Podcasts in the COVID-19 Transition to Virtual Post-Secondary Education in Agriculture'. *Natural Sciences Education* 50 (2), e20064.

Bartle, Emma, Nancy Longnecker, and Mark Pegrum. 2011. 'Collaboration, Contextualisation and Communication Using New Media: Introducing Podcasting into an Undergraduate Chemistry Class'. *International Journal of Innovation in Science and Mathematics Education* 19 (1): 16–28.

Bell, Stephanie. 2019. 'Learner-Created Podcasts: Fostering Information Literacies in a Writing Course'. *Canadian Journal for Studies in Discourse and Writing/Rédactologie* 29 (July): 51–63. doi: 10.31468/cjsdwr.747.

Berg, Freja Sørine Adler. 2021. 'Independent Podcasts on the Apple Podcast Platform in the Streaming Era'. *MedieKultur: Journal of Media and Communication Research* 37 (70): 110–30.

Berry, Richard. 2016a. 'Podcasting: Considering the Evolution of the Medium and Its Association with the Word "Radio"'. *Radio Journal: International Studies in Broadcast & Audio Media* 14 (1): 7–22.

———. 2016b. 'Part of the Establishment: Reflecting on 10 Years of Podcasting as an Audio Medium'. *Convergence* 22 (6): 661–71. doi: 10.1177/1354856516632105.

———. 2019. 'Mapping Podcasts'. *Richard Berry (blog)*. 28 December 2019. http://richardberry.eu/mapping-podcasts/.

———. 2020. 'Teaching Podcasts: Reflections on Recent Experience'. *Richard Berry (blog)*. 2 February 2020. https://richardberry.eu/teaching-podcasts-reflections-on-recent-experience/.

Besser, Erin D., Lauren E. Blackwell, and Matthew Saenz. 2021. 'Engaging Students through Educational Podcasting: Three Stories of Implementation'. *Technology, Knowledge and Learning* 26: 1–16.

Bolinches, Raúl Terol, and Nadia Alonso-López. 2021. 'Podcasting as a Tool to Make Online Academic Dissemination More Visible'. In *Improving University Reputation through Academic Digital Branding*, edited by Ariana Daniela Del Pino and Nuria Lloret Romero, 248–61. Hershey: IGI Global.

Bolliger, Doris U., Supawan Supanakorn, and Christine Boggs. 2010. 'Impact of Podcasting on Student Motivation in the Online Learning Environment'. *Computers & Education* 55 (2): 714–22. doi: 10.1016/j.compedu.2010.03.004.

Bossetta, Michael. 2020. 'The Professional Benefits of Podcasting Politics'. *PS: Political Science & Politics* 53 (2): 328–9. doi: 10.1017/S1049096519001628.

Brown, Heath, and Lilly J. Goren. 2020. 'The Personal Is Political: Podcasting Political Science'. *PS: Political Science & Politics* 53 (2): 322–3. doi: 10.1017/S1049096519001653.

Carvalho, Ana Amélia Amorim, Cristina Aguiar, and Romana Maciel. 2009. 'A Taxonomy of Podcasts and Its Application to Higher Education'. ALT-C 2009: In dreams begins responsability: choice, evidence and change: proceedings of the International Conference for the Association for Learning Technology, 16, Manchester, UK, 2009. [Manchester]: ALT, 2009. ISBN 978 0 95 458 709 3. pp. 132–140.

Casares Jr, D. Robert, and Erin E. Binkley. 2021. 'Podcasts as an Evolution of Bibliotherapy'. *Journal of Mental Health Counseling* 43 (1): 19–39.

Chan, Anthony, Mark J. W. Lee, and Catherine McLoughlin. 2006. 'Everyone's Learning with Podcasting: A Charles Sturt University Experience'. Proceedings of the 23rd annual ASCILITE conference: Who's learning? Whose technology? The University of Sydney, 110–20.

Church, Jeffrey. 2020. 'In Defense of the Long, Long Interview'. *PS: Political Science & Politics* 53 (2): 323–4. doi: 10.1017/S1049096519001616.

Cook, Ian M. 2018. 'How Podcasting Can Help Us Rethink Higher Education'. *Times Higher Education (THE)*. 12 November 2018. https://www.timeshighereducation.com/blog/how-podcasting-can-help-us-rethink-higher-education.

———— 2020. 'Critique of Podcasting as an Anthropological Method'. *Ethnography*. October 2020. doi: 10.1177/1466138120967039.

Cook, Ian M., and Sahana Udupa. 2019. 'Talking Media with "Online Gods": What Is Academic Podcasting Like?'. *Economic and Political Weekly* 54 (4): 7–8.

Cooper, Steve, Crispin Dale, and Steve Spencer. 2009. 'A Tutor in Your Back Pocket: Reflections on the Use of IPods and Podcasting in an Undergraduate Popular Music Programme'. *British Journal of Music Education* 26 (1): 85–97. doi: 10.1017/S0265051708008280.

Cotter, Christopher R., and David G. Robertson. 2021. 'Critique and Community: Podcasting Religious Studies'. In *Digital Humanities and Research Methods in Religious Studies Volume 2*, edited by C. D. Cantwell, and K. Petersen, 273–90. Berlin: De Gruyter.

Dominguez, Casey B. K., Cory Charles Gooding, and Timothy W. McCarty. 2020. 'A Few Reasonable Words'. *PS: Political Science & Politics* 53 (2): 325–6. doi: 10.1017/S1049096519001665.

Drew, Christopher. 2017a. 'Educational Podcasts: A Genre Analysis'. *E-Learning and Digital Media* 14 (4): 201–11.

————. 2017b. 'Edutaining Audio: An Exploration of Education Podcast Design Possibilities'. *Educational Media International* 54 (1): 48–62. doi: 10.1080/09523987.2017.1324360.

Eringfeld, Simone. 2021. 'Higher Education and Its Post-Coronial Future: Utopian Hopes and Dystopian Fears at Cambridge University during Covid-19'. *Studies in Higher Education* 46 (1): 146–57.

Euritt, Alyn. 2020. 'Within the Wires' Intimate Fan-Based Publics'. *Gender Forum* 77: 32–50.

Evans, Alice. 2020. '"Rocking Our Priors": Fun, Enthusiastic, Rigorous, and Gloriously'. *PS: Political Science & Politics* 53 (2): 320–2. doi: 10.1017/S1049096519001598.

Fantini, Emanuele, and Emilie Buist. 2021. 'Searching for the Sources of the Nile through a Podcast: What Did We Find?'. *Journal of Science Communication* 20 (2): N01. doi: 10.22323/2.20020801.

Fernandez, Vicenc, Pep Simo, and Jose M. Sallan. 2009. 'Podcasting: A New Technological Tool to Facilitate Good Practice in Higher Education'. *Computers & Education* 53 (2): 385–92. doi: 10.1016/j.compedu.2009.02.014.

Ferrer, Ilyan, Jessica Shaw, and Liza Lorenzetti. 2021. 'Ethical Storytelling and Digital Narratives: Lessons Learned in Student-Led Podcasts and Community Radio Partnerships'. *Journal of Social Work Values and Ethics* 18 (1): 90–104.

Fox, Matthew P., Kareem Carr, Lucy D'Agostino McGowan, Eleanor J. Murray, Bertha Hidalgo, and Hailey R. Banack. 2021. 'Will Podcasting and Social Media Replace Journals and Traditional Science Communication? No, But…'. *American Journal of Epidemiology* 190(8): 1625–31.

Frydenberg, Mark. 2008. 'Principles and Pedagogy: The Two Ps of Podcasting in the Information Technology Classroom'. *Information Technology* 11.

Gamwell, Adam. 2018. 'Talking Anthropology: Podcasting for the Public (Part One) | Teaching Culture'. 2018. http://www.utpteachingculture.com/talking-anthropology-podcasting-for-the-public-part-one/.

Grossmann, Matt. 2020. 'The Science of Politics Podcast'. *PS: Political Science & Politics* 53 (2): 324–5. doi: 10.1017/S1049096519001604.

Harter, Lynn M. 2019. 'Storytelling in Acoustic Spaces: Podcasting as Embodied and Engaged Scholarship'. *Health Communication* 34 (1): 125–29. doi: 10.1080/10410236.2018.1517549.

Heilesen, Simon B. 2010. 'What Is the Academic Efficacy of Podcasting?' *Computers & Education* 55 (3): 1063–8. doi: 10.1016/j.compedu.2010.05.002.

Herman, Eti, and David Nicholas. 2019. 'Scholarly Reputation Building in the Digital Age: An Activity-Specific Approach'. *El Profesional de La Informacion* 28 (1).

Hitchcock, Laurel Iverson, Todd Sage, Michael Lynch, and Melanie Sage. 2021. 'Podcasting as a Pedagogical Tool for Experiential Learning in Social Work Education'. *Journal of Teaching in Social Work* 41 (2): 172–91.

Jella, Tarun K., Thomas B. Cwalina, Alexander J. Acuña, Linsen T. Samuel, and Atul F. Kamath. 2021. 'Good Morning, Orthopods: The Growth and Future Implications of Podcasts in Orthopaedic Surgery'. *JBJS* 103 (9): 840–7.

Kamal, Salmaan, Shreya P. Trivedi, Utibe R. Essien, and Saman Nematollahi. 2021. 'Podcasting: A Medium for Amplifying Racial Justice Discourse, Reflection, and Representation within Graduate Medical Education'. *Journal of Graduate Medical Education* 13 (1): 29–32.

Kemp, Justine, Antony Mellor, Richard Kotter, and Jan W. Oosthoek. 2012. 'Student-Produced Podcasts as an Assessment Tool: An Example from Geomorphology'. *Journal of Geography in Higher Education* 36 (1): 117–30. doi: 10.1080/03098265.2011.576754.

Killean, Rachel, and Richard Summerville. 2020. 'Creative Podcasting as a Tool for Legal Knowledge and Skills Development'. *The Law Teacher* 54 (1): 31–42. doi: 10.1080/03069400.2019.1568675.

Law-Penrose, Jared. 2021. 'Reducing Uncertainty and Podcasting Engagement: An HR Classroom Response to COVID-19'. *Journal of Teaching and Learning with Technology* 10 (1): 365–72.

Lazzari, Marco. 2009. 'Creative Use of Podcasting in Higher Education and Its Effect on Competitive Agency'. *Computers & Education* 52 (1): 27–34. doi: 10.1016/j.compedu.2008.06.002.

Lee, Mark J. W., and Anthony Chan. 2007. 'Reducing the Effects of Isolation and Promoting Inclusivity for Distance Learners through Podcasting'. *Turkish Online Journal of Distance Education* 8 (1). doi: 10.17718/tojde.54987.

Lindgren, Mia. 2016. 'Personal Narrative Journalism and Podcasting'. *Radio Journal: International Studies in Broadcast & Audio Media* 14 (1): 23–41.

———. 2017. 'Autoethnographic Journalism – Subjectivity and Emotion in Audio Storytelling'. In *Reconstructing Identity: Reconstructing Identity: A Transdisciplinary Approach*, edited by N. Monk, M. Lindgren, S. McDonald, S. Pasfield-Neofitou. Cham: Palgrave Macmillan. doi: 10.1007/978-3-319-58427-0_9.

———. 2018. 'Researching Podcast Production – An Australian Podcast Study about Women and Work in Are We There Yet?'. In *Transnationalizing Radio Research: New Approaches to an Old Medium*, edited by Golo Föllmer and Alexander Badenoch, 283–91. Edition Medienwissenschaft, volume 42. Bielefeld: Transcript.

Llinares, Dario. 2018a. 'Podcasting as Liminal Praxis: Aural Mediation, Sound Writing and Identity'. In *Podcasting: New Aural Cultures and Digital Media*, edited by Dario Llinares, Neil Fox, and Richard Berry, 123–45. Cham: Palgrave Macmillan.

———. 2018b. *Podcasting: New Aural Cultures and Digital Media*. Cham: Palgrave Macmillan.

Llinares, Dario, Neil Fox, and Richard Berry. 2018. 'Introduction: Podcasting and Podcasts-Parameters of a New Aural Culture'. In *Podcasting: New Aural Cultures and Digital Media*, edited by Dario Llinares, Neil Fox, and Richard Berry, 1–13. Cham: Palgrave Macmillan.

Lonn, Steven, and Stephanie D. Teasley. 2009. 'Podcasting in Higher Education: What Are the Implications for Teaching and Learning?'. *The Internet and Higher Education*, Special Issue of the AERA Teaching and Learning Online Special Interest Group, 12 (2): 88–92. doi: 10.1016/j.iheduc.2009.06.002.

Lowe, Robert J., Matthew W. Turner, and Matthew Y. Schaefer. 2021. 'Dialogic Research Engagement through Podcasting as a Step towards Action Research: A Collaborative Autoethnography of Teachers Exploring Their Knowledge and Practice'. *Educational Action Research* 29: 1–18.

Lundström, Markus, and Tomas Poletti Lundström. 2020. 'Podcast Ethnography'. *International Journal of Social Research Methodology* 0 (0): 1–11. doi: 10.1080/13645579.2020.1778221.

Markman, Kris M. 2015. 'Considerations – Reflections and Future Research. Everything Old Is New Again: Podcasting as Radio's Revival'. *Journal of Radio & Audio Media* 22 (2): 240–3. doi: 10.1080/19376529.2015.1083376.

McCarthy, Shannon, Mark Pelletier, and Anna McCoy. 2021. 'Talking Together: Using Intercollegiate Podcasts for Increased Engagement in Marketing Education'. *Marketing Education Review* 31: 1–6.

McHugh, Siobhán. 2007. 'The Aerobic Art of Interviewing'. *Asia Pacific Media Educator* 18: 147–54.

———. 2012a. 'Oral History and the Radio Documentary/ Feature: Introducing the "COHRD" Form'. *Radio Journal: International Studies in Broadcast & Audio Media* 10 (1): 35–51. doi: 10.1386/rjao.10.1.35_1.

———. 2012b. 'The Affective Power of Sound: Oral History on Radio'. *The Oral History Review* 39 (2): 187–206. doi: 10.1093/ ohr/ohs092.

———. 2014. 'Audio Storytelling: Unlocking the Power of Audio to Inform, Empower and Connect'. *Asia Pacific Media Educator* 24 (2): 141–56. doi: 10.1177/1326365X14555277.

———. 2016. 'How Podcasting Is Changing the Audio Storytelling Genre'. *Radio Journal: International Studies in Broadcast & Audio Media* 14 (1): 65–82. doi: 10.1386/rjao.14.1.65_1.

———. 2022. *The Power of Podcasting: Telling Stories through Sound.* Sydney: NewSouth Books.

McHugh, S., I. McLean, and M. Neale. 2020. 'Notes from a Cross-Cultural Frontier: Investigating Australian Aboriginal Art through Podcasts.' *Liminalities: A Journal of Performance Studies* 16 (4). http://liminalities.net/16-4/podcasts.pdf.

McNamara, Scott, and Christopher Drew. 2019. 'Concept Analysis of the Theories Used to Develop Educational Podcasts'. *Educational Media International* 56 (4): 300–12. doi: 10.1080/09523987.2019.1681107.

McNamara, Scott W. T., and Justin A. Haegele. 2020. 'Undergraduate Students' Experiences with Educational Podcasts to Learn about Inclusive and Integrated Physical Education'. *European Physical Education Review*, June. doi: 10.1177/1356336X20932598.

Middleton, Andrew. 2009. 'Beyond Podcasting: Creative Approaches to Designing Educational Audio'. *ALT-J* 17 (2): 143–55. doi: 10.1080/09687760903033082.

Mooney, Julie A. 2019. 'Podcasting as Faculty Development Medium and Method: The Story of a Podcast Series Showcasing Teaching Excellence in Higher Education'. *Transformative Dialogues: Teaching & Learning Journal* 12 (2): 18.

Nelson, Robert J. 2021. 'Podcasting Services in Academic Libraries: A Case Study'. *College & Undergraduate Libraries*, 27: 1–16.

Nie, Ming, Alejandro Armellini, Sue Harrington, Kelly Barklamb, and Ray Randall. 2010. 'The Role of Podcasting in Effective Curriculum Renewal'. *ALT-J* 18 (2): 105–18. doi: 10.1080/09687769.2010.492849.

O'Connor, Siobhan, Claire S. Daly, Juliet MacArthur, Gunilla Borglin, and Richard G. Booth. 2020. 'Podcasting in Nursing and Midwifery Education: An Integrative Review'. *Nurse Education in Practice*, July, 102827. doi: 10.1016/j.nepr.2020. 102827.

Oslawski-Lopez, Jamie, and Gregory Kordsmeier. 2021. '"Being Able to Listen Makes Me Feel More Engaged": Best Practices for Using Podcasts as Readings'. *Teaching Sociology*. doi: 10.1177/0092055X211017197.

Pasquini, Laura. 2018. 'Pod Save Higher Ed: Resources for Podcasting'. *TechKNOWtools (blog)*. 22 October 2018. https:// techknowtools.com/2018/10/22/pod-save-highered/.

Pegrum, Mark, Emma Bartle, and Nancy Longnecker. 2015. 'Can Creative Podcasting Promote Deep Learning? The Use of Podcasting for Learning Content in an Undergraduate Science Unit: Creative Podcasting'. *British Journal of Educational Technology* 46 (1): 142–52. doi: 10.1111/bjet.12133.

Ralph, Jason, Naomi Head, and Simon Lightfoot. 2010. 'Pol-Casting: The Use of Podcasting in the Teaching and Learning of Politics and International Relations'. *European Political Science* 9 (1): 13–24. doi: 10.1057/eps.2009.38.

Ralph, Jaya, and Sonja Olsen. 2007. 'Podcasting as an Educational Building Block in Academic Libraries'. *Australian Academic & Research Libraries* 38 (4): 270–9. doi: 10.1080/00048623.2007.10721309.

Riecken, Ted. 2015. 'Mapping the Fit between Research and Multimedia: A Podcast Exploration of the Place of Multimedia Within / As Scholarship'. *McGill Journal of Education / Revue Des Sciences de l'éducation de McGill* 49 (3). https://mje.mcgill. ca/article/view/9061.

Rodman, Adam, Hannah R. Abrams, Matthew Watto, Shreya Trivedi, Jeff Barbee, Alejandro Meraz-Munoz, and Martin C. Fried. 2021. 'Medical Podcasting in Low- and Middle-Income Countries: A Needs Assessment and Vision for the Future'. *Teaching and Learning in Medicine* 33: 1–7.

Rogers, Dallas, Miles Herbert, Carolyn Whitzman, Eugene McCann, Paul J. Maginn, Beth Watts, Ashraful Alam, et al. 2020. 'The City under COVID-19: Podcasting as Digital Methodology'. *Tijdschrift Voor Economische En Sociale Geografie* 111 (3): 434–50. doi: 10.1111/tesg.12426.

Salvati, Andrew J. 2015. 'Podcasting the Past: Hardcore History, Fandom, and DIY Histories'. *Journal of Radio & Audio Media* 22 (2): 231–9. doi: 10.1080/19376529.2015.1083375.

Sciubba, Jennifer D. 2020. 'Podcasting Politics in an Era of Fatigue'. *PS: Political Science & Politics* 53 (2): 327–8. doi: 10.1017/S1049096519001641.

Seraydar, Sara, Samira Ebarhim Pour Komleh, and Mrayam Safar Navadeh. 2021. 'The Impact of Using Podcasts Academic Achievement, Learning Motivation and Creative Learning of Students in Fifth Grade's Elementary School Social Studies'. *Information and Communication Technology in Educational Sciences* 11 (44): 67–88.

Shamburg, Christopher. 2021. 'Rising Waves in Informal Education: Women of Color with Educationally Oriented Podcasts'. *Education and Information Technologies* 26 (1): 699–713.

Singer, Jonathan Bentley. 2019. 'Podcasting as Social Scholarship: A Tool to Increase the Public Impact of Scholarship and Research'. *Journal of the Society for Social Work and Research* 10 (4): 571–90. doi: 10.1086/706600.

Spinelle, Jenna. 2019. 'Why 2019 Will Be the Year of the Podcast in Higher Education — and What It Means for the Industry'. *Medium (blog)*. 6 January 2019. https://medium.com/age-of-awareness/why-2019-will-be-the-year-of-the-podcast-in-higher-education-and-what-it-means-for-the-industry-281eb7bb22ac.

Spinelli, Martin, and Lance Dann. 2019. *Podcasting: The Audio Media Revolution*. New York: Bloomsbury.

Strickland, Bronson K., Jarred M. Brooke, Mitchell T. Zischke, and Marcus A. Lashley. 2021. 'Podcasting as a Tool to Take Conservation Education Online'. *Ecology and Evolution* 11 (8): 3597–606.

Sullivan, John L. 2019. 'The Platforms of Podcasting: Past and Present'. *Social Media + Society* 5 (4). doi: 10.1177/2056305119880002.

Sundgren, Marcus. 2017. 'Blurring Time and Place in Higher Education with Bring Your Own Device Applications: A Literature Review'. *Education and Information Technologies* 22 (6): 3081–119. doi: 10.1007/s10639-017-9576-3.

Tysinger, Jeff A., and Dawn P. Tysinger. 2021. 'Podcasting as an Instructional Method: Case Study of a School Psychology Class'. *International Journal of Psychological and Behavioral Sciences* 15 (4): 432–37.

Van Zanten, Rob, Somogyi, Simon, and Gina Curro. 2012. 'Purpose and Preference in Educational Podcasting'. *British Journal of Educational Technology* 43 (1): 130–8. doi: 10.1111/j.1467-8535.2010.01153.x.

Wake, Alex, Kim Fox, and Catherine Strong. 2020. 'Pandemic Podcasting: From Classroom to Bedroom'. *Teaching Journalism & Mass Communication* 10 (1): 29–33.

Weimer, Kristina R. 2021. 'An Intrinsic Case Study of One Music Educator's Professional Development through Podcasting.' *Contributions to Music Education* 46: 245–63.

Williams, Adrienne E., Nancy M. Aguilar-Roca, and Diane K. O'Dowd. 2016. 'Lecture Capture Podcasts: Differential Student Use and Performance in a Large Introductory Course'. *Educational Technology Research and Development* 64 (1): 1–12. doi: 10.1007/s11423-015-9406-5.

Williams, Leonard. 2020. 'Political Science and Podcasts: An Introduction'. *PS: Political Science & Politics* 53: 319–20.

Index